WITHDRAWN

THE CASE FOR HEAVEN

Near-Death Experiences as
Evidence of the Afterlife

The
CASE
for
HEAVEN

*Near-Death Experiences as
Evidence of the Afterlife*

MALLY COX-CHAPMAN

G. P. Putnam's Sons   New York

G. P. PUTNAM'S SONS
Publishers Since 1838
200 Madison Avenue
New York, NY 10016

Library of Congress Cataloging-in-Publication Data

Cox-Chapman, Mally, date.
    The case for heaven : near-death experiences as evi-
dence of the afterlife / by Mally Cox-Chapman.
        p.   cm.
    Includes bibliographical references.
    ISBN 0-399-14024-7 (alk. paper)
    1. Near-death experiences—Religious aspects.
2. Future life.   3. Heaven.   I. Title.
BL535.C69   1995   94-46671 CIP
133.9'01'3—dc20

Book design by Marysarah Quinn

Printed in the United States of America
10 9 8 7 6 5 4 3 2 1

This book is printed on acid-free paper. ∞

Salutation

I salute you! There is nothing I can give you which you have not:
but there is much that, while I cannot give, you can take.

No heaven can come to us unless our hearts find rest in it today.
Take Heaven.

No peace lies in the future which is not hidden in this present
instant. Take peace.

The gloom of the world is but a shadow; behind it, yet within our
reach, is joy. Take joy.

—FRA GIOVANNI, 1513

Acknowledgments

This book owes its heart to the experiencers who gave their time and trusted that their story would be honored. I hope they will feel proud to have participated. What follows is the list of contributors, both experiencers and others, who added to my understanding, but who were not mentioned for various reasons in the text. (Others have chosen for personal reasons not to be mentioned here.) I wish to thank Denise Wade, Jean Sorensen-LeLoup, Margaret Walls, Patricia Bryson, Rick Bach, Alicia Skye, Evangeline Lincoln, Dianna Christenson, Nancy Kruger, Molly Morris, Cynthia Locke Day, Mimi Marie Cardwell,

Muriel Freifeld, Bill Taylor, Doug MacKenzie, and Sheryll Bedingfield-DiBell.

While not a scholarly work, this book has relied on the expertise of others. The scholars mentioned here have been patient with my questions and forthcoming with their knowledge: Bruce Greyson and Ronald Mallett at the University of Connecticut, David Kerr, William McKinney, and Miriam Therese Winter at the Hartford Seminary, Ronald Kiener at Trinity College, and David Kelsey at Yale Divinity School. On various religious questions I have turned to Rev. Elizabeth Fisher, Rev. Peter Grandy, and Dr. Lakshmi Sarma.

My thanks go to Lary Bloom and Jan Winburn at the *Hartford Courant* for publishing my first article on Heaven, and to the Hartford Seminary for holding a symposium in response to that article. On medical issues, Dr. Harry C. Weinerman and Dr. Robert D. Massey were good enough to read several chapters, and to be "on call" for checking medical facts. Any mistakes that remain are my own. Within IANDS (The International Association of Near-Death Studies), Dr. Michael Sabom, Jayne Smith, Jan Devereaux, and Jenny Greyson have provided well-timed insight and thoughtful arguments.

I have leaned on the resourceful librarians of the University of Connecticut Health Center Library, the Mortensen Library at the University of Hartford, and the West Hartford Public Library. I am particularly indebted to Rev. Lee Ellenwood at the John P. Webster Library, who fielded even the most arcane questions with good humor and erudition.

Not all books in the bibliography are created equal. My copies of *Otherworld Journeys,* by Carol Zaleski, *Heaven: A History,* by Colleen McDannell and Bernhard Lang, and Morton Kelsey's *Afterlife* are dog-eared and underlined. Stud Terkel's *Working* has been an inspiration all my professional life for its commitment to the power of people to speak their singular truths.

Thanks to Joanna Foggie, Stephanie Ferry, Karen Keller, Isabella Iapichino Marandino, Brenda Townsend, and everyone at Asylum Hill Church for all their moral support. Special thanks, too, to Kathy Schultz and David Paul, Joe Dworetzky, Sally Wister, Pauline Lavallee, Jo and Coleman Casey, Steve Goddard, Margie Michalski, Brie Quinby, and Sara Hadden. Such good friends they have been. And here's to the loyal opposition: Charlie Todd and Evan Cowles. Also to David Sessions, Ellsworth and Virginia Grant, Jan Mueller, Alan Mendelson, and Sam McKay for their generous gifts of office space—and good cheer.

For their early belief in me as a writer, my heartfelt thanks to the Breadloaf Writers' Conference and to Michael Curtis of the *Atlantic Monthly*. This book would not have happened without the steadfast support of my agent, John Ware, and the enthusiasm and energy of my editor, Stacy Creamer. I have relied on her assistant, Heather Clay, for technical advice and her talent for staying calm.

I was blessed with three mentors who read the manuscript in all its stages. Their knowledge and insight is surpassed only by the size of their hearts: Ruth Grobe, Nancy Bush, and Rev. Jim Kidd.

I am grateful to my beloved children, Jay and Lucy, who each in their dear way let me write this book. My deepest gratitude goes to my husband, Jim. My first book was dedicated to him; he was even more key to this one. To him, soulmate now and forever, thank you.

Contents

Preface

I have always believed in Heaven. My grandmother told me lovely stories about it when I was little before I went to sleep at night, and I believed every one of them. As an adult, however, I was embarrassed to admit it. Notions of Heaven seemed so innocent, so intellectually tacky. Astronauts proved it was not in the sky, and Freud reduced it to wishful thinking. So why am I writing this book?

Ten years ago I was driving on a rain-slicked road in Philadelphia that winds along the Schukyll River. Putting my foot on the brakes set the car into a spin. As the car began to roll, a clear, comforting voice coming from the sun visor on the passenger side said, without words, "Relax. It is not your time to die."

I obeyed immediately, letting my body go floppy. When my car came to a stop facing the river, other cars screeched to a halt. Drivers came running to pull me from the car. I was completely serene; my heart was not even pounding. I asked about the well-being of the other drivers, wiped off the worst of the mud and clumps of grass caught on the windows, and drove home.

Some psychologists would say that I experienced depersonalization, that part of my own unconscious told me what to do. Others, more religiously inclined, might describe what happened as an angel experience. I now believe that at a moment of high peril when death was eminently possible, my spirit was allowed to connect with another dimension of reality.

Whatever the explanation, one thing seemed certain—and new: if it was not my time to die, it was my time to live. Every day was a precious gift.

At the time of the accident, I had been married for nine years but had been postponing having children. Within a month, I was pregnant. At the time of the accident, I was at a dead end in my career. Within a year I had switched into feature journalism, writing articles on the human condition. And where I had felt that notions of Heaven were intellectually tacky, I now felt I had sure knowledge of one of its messengers.

By any measure, my experience was thin. This book will describe far more remarkable accounts of experiencers (as they are commonly called) hovering thousands of feet above car accidents, shooting through tunnels at the speed of light for reunions with loved ones who have died, and going through life reviews in the presence of divine judges.

Experiencers are a generous and forthcoming group whose lives have often been radically transformed by their glimpse of

Heaven's light. I am grateful for the chance to tell their stories. The book is based on fifty-one interviews, against a background of intensive research in the field. Fewer than 10 percent of their accounts had to be put aside because in one way or another those experiences were atypical. By and large, near-death experiences have a focal point. Five out of the fifty-one experiences are so profound, however, that they convey multiple messages and will be mentioned throughout the book.

The experiencers in this book are average people. Included, for instance, are nurses, secretaries, an airline pilot, a professor of philosophy, homemakers, people in business, and a driving instructor. They are bringing up children, holding down jobs, enjoying the goodness of life when they can. The difference is that they have had a brush with death during which something happened to them that is emotional, internal, and subjective—and echoes the experience of millions of others.

So bring whatever doubts you have with you, but do not let them own you. The experiencers who tell their stories on these pages join me in the hope that in reading this book, your own fear of death will be alleviated, and that you will come closer to the deep understanding that experiencers have of Heaven.

THE CASE FOR HEAVEN

Near-Death Experiences as
Evidence of the Afterlife

Chapter 1

What Can Near-Death Experiences Reveal about Heaven?

. . . and we have no evidence whatsoever that the soul perishes with the body.

—MAHATMA GANDHI

Heaven is real.

Wouldn't it be wonderful to know that? Can you imagine how you would feel with certain knowledge of life beyond death?

A group of parishioners at a small country church were listening to a talk on Heaven when a short, heavyset policewoman named Dorothy Young raised her hand. She told the congregation that she knew there was a Heaven because she had been there. She had been in the hospital in the process of miscarrying her fourth child when she felt a cold, dark chill pass over her. Suddenly she was surrounded by a warm, bright light that totally enveloped her. She felt happier than she ever had before. It was utterly quiet, she said, "a quiet without shadows or walls." She heard the sound of a baby crying deep in the Light. She was given to understand that her stillborn daughter was going to stay in the Light and that she was fine.

When Dorothy "came back" from the gray mist where she had heard her baby, a sheet was over her head. She had been pronounced dead. When she pulled the sheet off her head, the nurse in the room shrieked and had to be sent home. Dorothy herself has never grieved for the baby who was born dead. She has a bone-deep conviction that because she was a mother to three other children, God pulled her back to finish her work on earth. She believes she will see her stillborn daughter in Heaven.

As Dorothy finished her account, the church group sat in stunned silence. This was not some stranger talking. This was Dorothy, the calm dispatcher at the police station, the one everyone called when there was a crisis in town. This was their neighbor.

Each person listening to Dorothy had to decide if her story was trustworthy. Each had to wonder what it meant. As Dorothy's own pastor said afterward, "I've never really paid much attention to near-death experiences. I thought of them as fodder for made-for-TV movies. But my godmother changed her life because of one, and now Dorothy's telling hers, and I'm thinking, 'This is really important.'"

An impressive number of Americans and people all over the world have had near-death experiences, or NDEs as they are commonly called. According to a Gallup poll, at least eight million people in America alone have had near-death experiences. Nearly all near-death experiencers have an unshakable belief in the afterlife.

The argument presented here is not religious in the traditional sense. There will be no discussion of Ten Commandments or Four Noble Truths, no guides to the Way to Live. But near-death experiencers function as a wellspring of collective religious revelation about Heaven. Experiencers are telling the people around them what they have learned. The power of their conviction is having an effect.

About half of the experiencers interviewed offered to tell their story after reading about this study in the newsletter for the International Association of Near-Death Studies (IANDS). The others heard about it through word-of-mouth. Most were interviewed twice.

Many more women than men volunteered for this project. As Dr. Kenneth Ring, a professor of psychology at the University of Connecticut and the dean of near-death research, has pointed out, although women are more willing to discuss their near-death experiences, his research indicates that there is no discernible difference between men and women in terms of the experiences themselves.

Only two of the experiencers asked to have their names changed, and both of those were for good reasons. One is a health-care professional who felt that her career would be jeopardized; the other had her near-death experience in connection with a rape and murder. Her assailant may still be at large.

Even when the stakes were not as high, many experiencers interviewed for this book admitted it felt risky to share their stories. Dorothy Young had told no one except her mother and best friend for fear of being judged as odd. But as public acceptance of near-death experiences grows, many of those eight million are telling family and friends what they have learned.

If a friend confided in you over tea late at night that she had had a near-death experience in which she went to Heaven, you would probably listen with respect, and maybe with wonder or skepticism, depending on your temperament. The story might or might not persuade you that there is "another side." But what if ten people told you similar stories over tea late at night? What if fifty friends confided such accounts? Eight million? At what point would their conviction become your religious question? At what point would you have to reconsider your own faith journey?

Sheer numbers would not usually be sufficiently persuasive. Many more than eight million people throughout history have believed in human sacrifice, yet few are inclined to accept such religious practices today. But Aztecs and Incas chose their beliefs. Experiencers have change foisted upon them. Dorothy, for example, grew up in a Christian family. One might assume that a revelation of Heaven would confirm joyfully her family's most dearly held beliefs. Instead, Dorothy has felt that her experience of Heaven put a difficult burden on her. She has lived with the uneasy feeling these past twenty-seven years that she ought to "do" something with her experience. She was supposed to be a messenger, but she did not know to whom. Dorothy hopes that by telling the group at church and through participation in this study that she will somehow have fulfilled her obligation.

Bettina Pratt, a tiny Bostonian lady in her sixties, has also told very few people about her experience. She contracted encephalomyelitis, a complication of measles, when she was nineteen. She remembers perceiving herself as hovering just below the ceiling of the infirmary room looking down on a doctor, a nurse, and the shape of her own body under the sheets. The nurse said, "I can't get a pulse" in a panicky voice.

Suddenly Bettina was on the edge of something she feels she cannot adequately describe. She says, "How can one describe a light that is very, very bright and very, very soft at the same time? I knew that it was living and loving and that I was going to get into it, and I could hardly wait. There wasn't any me anymore. I didn't have a body, and yet I didn't hurt. I should have hurt, but it was so bright I was awed and overjoyed, and I knew where I was and why. I call it heavenly, because that's the best word we've got. It was bliss."

This experience had a profound effect on Bettina's life. Her fear of death, which had caused nightmares all her life, was gone forever. She has spent much of her life learning about spirituality and Eastern mysticism as a way to understand what happened to her as a teenager.

Bettina's experience, like Dorothy's, creates a methodological problem: her NDE is self-reported and cannot be verified objectively. Death or its relative nearness is sometimes hard to define. Visits to the edge of Heaven cannot be proved. Some researchers have found that an experience can occur even when the closeness of death is not clear. Experiencers themselves almost always speak of themselves as being dead, and they have reasonable corroborative evidence to back up their claim. Only those interviewees whose proximity to death was persuasive have been included. In fact, medical understanding is making it increasingly clear that there is no such thing as a moment of death. If dying is a process, the soul may intersect with another plane of reality anywhere along a continuum.[1] Like explorers standing on a hillside with binoculars, near-death experiencers glimpse our common destiny.

There are, of course, skeptics who try to dismiss near-death experiences. They contend that drugs, oxygen deprivation, or disassociation caused the experience. Temporal lobe stimulation, endorphin surge, anesthesia, and even memories of birth have also been proposed as the reasons for the experiences. The consensus of researchers in the field is that there are probably various triggers for near-death experiences. Some are yet to be discovered. But each one of the possible causes has an argument against it.[2] One of Dr. Kenneth Ring's earliest findings, for example, was that anesthesia actually cuts down on the likelihood of patients' re-membering an NDE, since medications such as Valium are usually added to the anesthetic recipe to create amnesia for the time of the operation.

Furthermore, a trigger is not the experience itself. We know that rapid eye movement, frequently called REM, triggers dreams. We know that the feeling of being in love is triggered by a surge of endorphins. But no matter how much we know about their neurochemistry, dreams and love have a reality far more powerful than the chemicals that cause them. The same is true for near-death experiences. NDEs need to be assessed not only by what causes them but also by the luminous consequences they have in experiencers' lives.

As Dr. Kenneth Ring has pointed out, there has been so much research done that we can definitely conclude that the NDE itself is authentic. Researchers have studied experiencers in Australia, India, South America, and England, to name only a few of the areas. Thousands of experiencers in this country have entered their names into the database of the International Association of Near-Death Studies. Although researchers disagree about how to interpret near-death experiences, they do not dispute that experiences occur.

Common characteristics of near-death experiences have been determined. Among them are: feelings of peace and quiet; feeling oneself out of the body; going through a dark tunnel; meeting others, including one or more Beings of Light; a life review; coming to a border or limit; coming back; seeing life differently; and having new views of death.

Not all experiences will contain all the attributes. Full-blown experiences are relatively rare. What follows is a theoretical experience that includes all the common elements. Although only a construct, it may help convey a sense of what happens during a near-death experience:

A woman is dying, and she knows it. Suddenly she hears an uncomfortable noise, a loud ringing or buzzing, and realizes that she is lifting out of her physical body. She may hover over her physical body watching resuscitation attempts or loved ones who are grieving. She may try, to no avail, to communicate with those below her, or attempt to reassure them that she is fine. Pain is gone. At the same time she feels herself moving rapidly through a long, dark tunnel.

On the other side of the tunnel, the experiencer takes time to get her bearings. She notices that the nature of her body has changed, but the change does not feel alarming. She may find herself in a gray mist or in a beautiful pastoral setting. Soon others come to meet and to help her. She sees relatives and friends who have already died. A loving, warm Being of Light dressed in long, white robes begins to communicate by telepathy. The experiencer is asked to evaluate her life and is shown a panoramic, instantaneous playback of her life. She then approaches a barrier or a border—it may be a stream, a fence, a stone wall—that she intuitively knows is the limit between earthly life and the next life. She must make the choice about whether to stay or go back to earth. Having never felt such love, joy, and acceptance before, she yearns to stay but realizes that her job on earth is not yet complete. The time for her death has not yet come. As soon as she makes that decision, she is instantly back in her body.

Later she tries to tell someone close to her, but no one seems to understand. When ridiculed, she learns to be quiet about it. Still, the experience transforms her life. She now believes that love and learning are the only things that matter. She completely and totally loses her fear of death and is convinced that she will participate in an afterlife.

What are we to think? Are these experiences trustworthy? Some researchers have concentrated on the out-of-body aspects of NDEs as a way to verify the experiences. If it could be proven, for example, that Bettina, hovering just below the ceiling of the infirmary room, could see things that she could not have seen from her bed, then her observations would constitute fair proof that an experiencer's soul can travel. Furthermore, experiencers make comments about such things as their doctors' bald spots seen from above and give opinions of remarks that were made in rooms down the hall while they were in severe comas.

Some of these out-of-body perceptions have been verified by independent witnesses. Madelaine Lawrence, R.N., Ph.D., Director of Nursing Research at Hartford Hospital, has reported some preliminary findings in an article in the *Journal of Near-Death Studies,* the scholarly publication of the International Association of Near-Death Studies. Hartford Hospital is doing a long-term study of coma, and all patients who have been in a coma are interviewed as soon as possible after they come out of it. The patient Lawrence cites in her article described floating up over her body and viewing the resuscitation effort being done on her. She then felt herself being pulled up through several floors of the hospital that seemed to dissolve as she moved through them until she found herself above the roof. She was enjoying the view of the night skyline of the city when, out of the corner of her eye, she saw a red object. It was a shoe. She thought about the shoe, and suddenly she felt "sucked up a blackened hole" into the rest of her near-death experience.

On her return into her body, the patient told her experience to a nurse, who told the story to a medical resident, who laughed. Luckily, the resident took his skepticism right upstairs to the janitor, convincing him to get a ladder. On checking, they did indeed find a red shoe in the gutter on the roof.[3]

Even as we are attracted to such stories, we search for explanations. But it seems highly unlikely that a woman brought in on the ground floor in an ambulance could have any knowledge of a red shoe on the roof.

One of the most cautious, and therefore most startling, studies of out-of-body experiences during near-death experiences was conducted by Dr. Michael Sabom, a cardiologist and staff physician at the Atlanta Veterans' Administration Medical Center who is one of the leading researchers in the near-death field. He asked thirty-two patients who claimed to have had an out-of-body experience (OBE) during a cardiac arrest to explain in detail what they thought the resuscitation effort had consisted of. He also asked a control group of twenty-five "seasoned" cardiac patients to hazard the same description. These patients had not claimed an out-of-body experience. The backgrounds of the control group were similar to those of the experiencers, and their condition would have attracted them to learning whatever they could about resuscitation—whether in television and films, or through questions put to medically knowledgeable informants. Most had already had a heart attack and four had had cardiac arrests without an NDE.

Twenty out of the twenty-five patients in the control group made a major error in their attempts to describe the resuscitation process. In the group of thirty-two who claimed to have watched the procedure from outside their bodies, on the other hand, there were no errors in the descriptions given. Twenty-six answered with a description that correlated in a general way with the known facts of their CPR. Six of the thirty-two near-death experiencers were able to recall very specific aspects of their resuscitation. They described such unlikely details as the gurneys they were pulled on, the shape of the paddles used, and which family members were waiting, frightened, down the hall.

The goal of both the scientific researchers who first published the red shoe account and of Dr. Sabom was to provide verification of an out-of-body experience. But what are the implications of out-of-body experiences? The Hartford researchers called the woman's consciousness her "energy center." Others might be inclined to call it her soul. When researchers can verify that the soul can see and travel beyond the body, we have gone a long way to proving that near-death experiences must be taken very seriously indeed.

The aftereffects are significant. Most come back believing that love and learning are what God wants of us, and they find themselves adjusting their lives to those mandates. Many experiencers change their self-image, their relationships, and their work. The change does not mean that they are better people than someone who has not had an experience. They are not necessarily more saintly. The difference is that they see their lives as opportunities for spiritual growth.

If experiencers were atheists before, they are believers afterward. If they had a firm commitment to one particular religion before, they believe any religious path leads to God afterward. And in study after study, conversation after conversation, they say that they absolutely believe that their souls will persist beyond physical death.

Near-death experiences are neither new nor exclusive to the United States. The deloks of Tibet are a splendid example of near-death visionaries who are little known in the West but are very familiar to Tibetans. Delok means "returned from death" in Tibetan. Traditionally deloks seem to die because of illness and are given entry into the "bardo" world, the transitional space in which Buddhists believe we travel before coming back into the next life. Deloks visit a bardo version of hell, are given judgments about their lives, and are frequently shown glimpses of heavenly realms. They are then awarded messages to bring back to the living. Often they are accompanied by a deity whose job it is to protect them and to explain what is happening.

The stories of historic deloks are written down as part of the Tibetan Buddhist tradition, and traveling minstrels sing the biographies of these deloks all over Tibet. As Sogyal Rinpoche, author of *The Tibetan Book of Living and Dying,* has pointed out, deloks often have a hard time persuading people that their story is true, "and they spend the rest of their lives recounting their experiences to others in order to draw them toward the path of wisdom."[4]

The tradition of honoring deloks continues in the Himalayas today. Deloks are not just some foreign oddity. Dorothy the policewoman is an American version of the delok. She told her story to her congregation, giving her wisdom to others and growing wiser herself in having the courage to tell it. Tibetans honor their deloks. It is time we in other traditions listen to our near-death experiencers for the spiritual insights they have about Heaven.

NOTES

1. See *Recollections at Death,* by Dr. Michael Sabom, for a cautious evaluation of this issue. Sabom insists that nearness to death matters. Sabom's book is currently out of print but available in many libraries.

2. For more detailed arguments rebutting the reductionist it's-nothing-but claims about near-death experiences, read Zaleski's *Otherworld Journeys,* pp. 163–83, or Dr. Melvin Morse's appendix on the subject in *Closer to the Light,* pp. 214–26.

3. Madelaine Lawrence and Kenneth Ring, "Journal of Near-Death Studies" 11, no 4: 227. I recommend becoming a member of IANDS and subscribing to the journal to anyone who is seriously interested in following the research in the field.

4. Sogyal Rinpoche, *The Tibetan Book of Living and Dying,* pp. 330–36.

Chapter 2

What Is Heaven Like?

The undiscovered country, from whose bourn
No traveler returns . . .

—WILLIAM SHAKESPEARE
HAMLET, ACT 3, SCENE 1

Miracles do not happen in contradiction to nature,
but only in contradiction to that which is known to
us in nature.

—AUGUSTINE

Once there was a president of Yale named Arthur Twining Hadley who was a brilliant connoisseur of wine. He was famous for his ability to name not only the type and year of a wine but also the vineyard where the grapes had ripened. The faculty looked everywhere for a wine with which to stump him. One evening at a faculty dinner, they challenged him to name the wine being served. Hadley sipped the wine and named it without hesitation. His faculty said no. He took another sip. Again the faculty said no. Four times Hadley guessed.

After the fourth try, the faculty conceded defeat. Hadley had succeeded in naming all four vineyards surrounding the field from which the wine had been produced, a vineyard from which no wine had ever been produced before.[1]

Heaven is like that vineyard. We human beings can gather a bounty of information and inspiration from all the fields surrounding Heaven. Religion, science, and now near-death experiences can take us right to the edge of insight. Near-death experiencers are simply people who believe that, through no choice of their own, they have traveled as close as anyone can to Heaven's ineffable field.

Mary Dooley is a fashion designer and fine-arts painter who describes her upbringing as sheltered by Victorian parents. She and her family avoided fortune-tellers, horoscopes, or anything that smacked of the occult. Although an avid reader, Mary carefully avoided anything that may have been cultist or unusual. That included the *Reader's Digest*! So Mary had never heard of near-death experiences when she entered the hospital for surgery for uterine cancer. She was thirty-four and had been married for eight months. She described her near-death experience in a letter. "I had entered the hospital for surgery and knew that a nurse friend, Irene, would be awaiting me in the recovery room. She was to attend me after the operation. The last thing that I remembered was praying. The anesthesia took over.

"Suddenly I found myself in a strange place. I recognized nothing. I was weightless and going very very fast with no exertion on my part. It was like I was floating, and I had the feeling I could fly if I cared to, but I didn't try. I was in a dark void in what appeared to be sort of a tunnel. I felt no fear as to what was happening to me. Then I realized that I was approaching a very bright light at the end of this tunnel. I remember thinking that I hadn't my sunglasses with me. My eyes had always been sensitive to light, and this concerned me. However, when I reached the brightness, I found no strain to my eyes, nor did I need any adjustment for the light. Though it was extremely bright, there was much softness to it. *Soothing* would be a good word."

In this first stage, Mary's tone is practical. She worries about forgetting her sunglasses and takes stock of the situation. Her tone changes to awe and excitement in the next section. "Then I saw the colors! There was every color of the rainbow plus colors I'd not ever seen before! It was so very beautiful and so ineffable. As things began to take shape for me I could see grasses, flowers, and the extreme beauty surrounding me. Oh yes, we do have beauty here on earth, but it was nothing compared to what I was seeing. It was truly a Heavenly place where I had found myself. I was so happy! I'd never want to leave all of this. I felt such a glow within me. I felt the presence of God. His radiance was everywhere. He *was* the light. It was emanating from Him! I remember thinking, "I have died! I am in Heaven! I made it! With all of my faults I made it! I felt unworthy of it, but I had made it.

"Looking to one side I saw what appeared to be a fence or wall about two feet high. It was covered with gems of every color and hue. Colors were softened, not garish. It had a gate that was covered the same way. Beyond this wall there were several people standing. Upon seeing them I *knew* they were heavenly beings. I recognized none of them, but I could feel their love toward me and my love toward them. Love was everywhere! I felt so at ease.

"We spoke no words to one another. We communicated with our minds in telepathy. They knew what I was thinking, and I knew what they were thinking. They asked if I would stay. Remember that I had wanted to stay, that I never wanted to leave. When the question was put to me, my whole life appeared to me in rapid order. It was like an old-time movie in very fast action. But it was me!—and can you imagine? They were giving me a choice! I then 'explained' that I was needed here; I had left much work undone. I, who had vowed never to leave, opted for it.

"Except for the swiftness of the tunnel and the fast view of my life, everything else seemed to go at an earthly pace. However, after my decision to leave, I felt an immediate jerk of my body and I could hear my nurse calling my name. When I opened my eyes, her first words to me were, 'You gave us a terrible scare.'"

What was Mary to make of her experience? She says she thought of telling her friend, the nurse Irene, what had happened, but there were too many people around. Mary was afraid they would think she was crazy. The only person she told, years later, was her daughter. She deeply regrets that she never told her husband, now deceased, about her experience. She believes that it would have alleviated his fear of death and brought them closer.

Mary's own fear of death disappeared. "As a matter of fact I look forward to it," she admitted in a follow-up interview. "That doesn't mean I wish it were today or tomorrow. It means the experience of dying and the love and beauty has yet to come, and I await it without fear."

Mary believes that when she dies she will go through the beautiful gate that she saw in her NDE. "I was in Heaven," she says, "but you have to go through the gate to get to the fun part."

Does Mary's experience teach us what the gate to Heaven looks like? Her experience certainly evokes many popular images of Heaven: angelic figures, a gate that, while not pearly, is close enough, and a Light and loving peace that, as the Bible would say, passeth all understanding. The pastoral setting, the expanses of grass and the soothing atmosphere are all found in the Muslim sacred text, the Qur'an.

If Mary had lived several thousand years ago, and had been willing to tell her experience, her experience might very well have been added to the religious canon of her tribe. As it is, Mary lives in a modern age when vast numbers of similar experiences are being collected and studied in a secular manner. The Mormons are an exception. Several Mormon researchers have recently published accounts of Mormon near-death experiences of Heaven that attest to a wide variety of plant life, colors such as we have never seen, and a beautiful city of lights where complicated music is composed and vast stores of knowledge are compiled. Does that mean that if we read these accounts we will know all about Heaven?

Not quite. Mary is modest in her reactions to her own NDE. She does not claim to know universal truth. She says that she was in Heaven but that "you have to go through the gate to get to the fun part." She is acknowledging that there are limits to what we can learn about the ineffable.

Experiencers describe their experience in their own cultural context. A truck driver said he shot through a tailpipe toward a brilliant light. A young mother called the Beings she met the "Spirit People" when she first recounted her experience; six months later, she had joined a church and was referring to them as Jesus and the angels. It is so human. We want our lives to conform with reality as we know it.

Marianne Helms grew up in Kansas. When she had a severe allergic reaction to a bee sting in 1958, she felt herself lift off from her body and head toward a white shining light. She felt eager, knowing that she would soon see her beloved deceased mother and Jesus. Marianne traveled up through an allee of trees such as line many of the major roads of western Europe. This makes sense given her frame of reference: Marianne has spent most of her adult life living in Geneva, Switzerland, where such allees are common.

Experiencers also describe their experiences in the context of their own religious background, or lack thereof. Christians will often identify the Being of Light that greets them as Christ, or other biblical figures. Jews will call them angels. A person who has had no religious training or conviction described him as he saw him: a Being of Light. None of the experiencers necessarily mean to imply that the Being had a human figure. The descriptions have in common a sense of there being a guide made of light. Religious labels are often then superimposed on that reality.[2]

This inclination is particularly transparent in the experience of Betty Jane Ramsey, a hardworking teacher with a master's degree in English whose life was changed by her near-death experience. At the time of her experience, she was a mother of two who had not finished high school.

Betty Jane had finally given up and left the music festival in Asheville, North Carolina, where her husband was master of ceremonies. She had been vomiting continuously for over twenty-four hours. She could not keep fluids down. By the next day her husband came home to be with their young daughters while her parents drove her to the Takoma Medical Group. Her stomach virus led to dehydration. She was given an injection.

Feeling weak, Betty Jane leaned on the counter of the medical center, waiting to pay her bill. Suddenly a burning, stinging pain radiated out from the site of the injection in her right hip to her entire body. Recalls Betty Jane, "It felt like a layer of fire beneath my skin."

Betty Jane blacked out. As she recalls in a written account: "My body was lying on the floor by the checkout counter, but I was not there. I just floated out of my body! I floated right up through the building. I could see the top of the building and the parking lot, the trees and houses, and my parents waiting in the car. I could see Greenville, Tennessee, as I went up over the trees.

"I felt this great peace and the most exquisite joy. I was floating right up through the clouds and the sky. I had a new body that felt so good. I was wearing something light and white. I did not remember earth. Not my husband; nor even my two small children. Not my parents; not my sisters. I did not remember the past; there were not thoughts of the future. It seemed like a very slow ascent.

"Finally, I came to the most beautiful land," says Betty Jane. "There was the most beautiful city I had ever seen. The buildings were different sizes, like a modern city, but they were all white."

Although the buildings seemed to be made of stone or concrete, they reminded Betty Jane of the whitewashed adobe architecture of Spanish cities. But the light was different, she says: "The light was soft, glowing, and warm. There were bells ringing and these bells pealed music like none on earth in sweetness. There were voices singing. The music and singing were like all the old masters of classical music rolled into one, come to perfection. Everything was very clear, no smog or pollution. There were tinkling sounds, like water running from a fountain. There was a radiance like the sun, but I don't remember seeing a sun.

"Then I saw Jesus and He was the most perfect creation of all. He was in perfect physical health. He was dressed in white and he was more radiant than any of the pictures in which He has been portrayed on earth. I have been asked if his skin was black or white and the strange thing is that I cannot remember. He reached out his hands to me and I reached mine for his, but at that moment, I began slipping back down. Down through the clouds, down through the sky, down through the building, and down into my body on the floor. The descent was with incredible speed. I began to feel as if I were in a soft bed with fluffy pillows and cozy, warm comforter—such peace with no pain."

Betty Jane's religious background is Missionary Baptist. When Betty Jane was asked in a follow-up interview how she could tell that it was Jesus who reached out to her, she mentioned his white robes and the love in his eyes. But then she interrupted herself to say she "just knew."

In their wide study of American and Indian deathbed visions,

Karlis Osis and Erlendur Haraldsson point out that American experiencers who see a radiant man clad in white are likely to interpret that figure as Jesus, God, or an angel. An Indian experiencer who is a Hindu, on the other hand, is more likely to interpret the figure as Krishna, Shiva, or Deva.

The fact that experiencers describe the world in the context that is most comfortable to them does not discredit the description. But it does mean that we must be very careful with revelations of Heaven in near-death experiences not to assume either that they are literal truth or merely metaphor. The experiencers participate in a great reality, but they are not the whole reality. Experiencers have stood, symbolically, at the edge of the vineyard, but that does not mean they know everything about the lay of the land.

Some experiencers believe that they are presented with images that are familiar to them during the NDE so that they can handle the overwhelming reality of what they are experiencing. The familiar images act as a kind of cosmic kindliness.

An experiencer named Mary Free found this to be true. A driving instructor who loves animals, she speaks with the strong twang of her home state, Texas. The facts of Mary's life at the time of her experience were bleak: it was the early seventies, her husband had just left her and their five young children, and she had a severe case of hepatitis and was too sick to get herself to the hospital.

In the account that she gave by phone, Mary's language has a disjointed quality. Experiencers tend to layer language—interrupting themselves, starting over—out of exasperation about getting it right.

"I felt my essence spin out of my body," Mary said. "I felt the warmth traveling up my body, and then I didn't feel anything. The next thing I know, I'm standing before a beautiful golden tree. I knew it was all of a different substance than a physical substance. Standing before it, I knew that the light was composed of life. These shining particles knew me. And they had the option; they could be bigger, or smaller. I noticed there is no evil here, no negativity. I felt very peaceful. I won a beauty contest when I was fourteen. Even without looking, I knew I was a thousand times more beautiful in my celestial body. If you looked at it [the golden tree] closely, there were all these pastel shapes of energy. I felt like I should just call it life. And they seemed like they were smiling back at me, all these little individuals. And they knew me. And there was so much happiness there.

"To my left and a little behind me, He approaches me. You could call him God or Jesus. I call him the Creator. Out of reverence, I suppose, I am not looking at Him. Later on He has to beckon me to look at Him. The closer He gets to me, the happier I am. He is beside me and behind me all at the same time. I asked Him if something I had done would keep me from Heaven. He laughed, totally without malice—loving, welcoming laughter. He had humor. I learned [that Heaven] is on hold for me. When I die here and go back there, I have ready access to it. It's exactly there even if I have eighty more years here. At the point I left off, I go right back to then."

During her near-death experience, Mary believes she was shown the nature of the universe by the Creator. The information was overwhelming. She wanted to go back to her children to guide them to adulthood. The Creator agreed, but before what she describes as the "departing process" began, Mary was given a last look at the golden tree.

As she recalls it, "The spot where the golden tree was had never left there. I realize now that the golden tree was a composite for me. For my own security I was shown the golden tree. It was not an illusion. It's not to say it's fake. It's real. But instead of going immediately into space, I was shown in stages."

Mary says that she would have been overwhelmed if the Creator had wanted her to look through the portal at the universe immediately. Seeing the golden tree first gave her a frame of reference, something, in the truest metaphysical sense, for her to lean on. In other words, the golden tree was a moment of cosmic kindliness. According to Mary, the golden tree may or may not be there when she returns.

Another experiencer discovered the same cosmic kindliness when she found her beloved deceased great aunt at the end of the tunnel. In the months that followed her experience, as she mulled over what her great aunt had taught her, it became increasingly clear to her that she had been in the presence of the holy. "God in an aunt suit," she says now. This dual role did nothing to diminish the joy of reunion with her great aunt. Rather, the experiencer is grateful that her revelation was expressed in a manner she could handle.

There are exceptions. Some experiencers are completely surprised by the manner of revelation in their otherworld journey. Charlene Grove was raped and strangled when she was twenty-two. The first stage of her near-death experience was horrifying. At the other end of the tunnel, however, everything changed.

"So what did I see? I didn't see what some people saw because I didn't go far enough. I was motionless. The Force was gone. I was absolutely motionless, free of everything. I was suspended high above an infinite sea of gridlike perfect cobblestones, laid out, endless. A sea of clouds. Or something."

Charlene's voice changed as she described the sea of clouds. She sounded calm and happy, as though describing the perfect summer day.

"It was patterned perfectly. There was no end and no beginning to it. I was above it. As a stewardess, I had seen clouds above the ocean. This was like an ocean or a sea of a patterned grid. As I looked down, they didn't look like anything I'd seen flying. They didn't look like this earth-cloud stuff. I just knew there was no end to it. This whole canopy was filled with salmon, gold, peach, and pale yellow-colored light.

"My feeling that I had in life up to that point about trying to make some meaning out of life, and why I was suffering so, I mean not just being kidnapped and raped . . . my whole life had been difficult. That was all gone. Chaos was gone. My emotions were at peace. I was free. Absolute silence, stillness, peace, and this order![sic] that was below me, I didn't know what it was, seemed to rule."

For most of us, the news that the afterlife was a pale gray grid stretching out forever would not be good news, no matter how beautifully suffused with salmon, gold, and peach-colored light. For Charlene, the vision she was given during her near-death experience has infused her life with meaning. It prompted a spiritual search that has brought joy to her life. While the aura of light and peace are similar to Betty Jane Ramsey's and Mary Dooley's near-death experiences, the geography is not.

The contrasts in these experiences implies that we must qualify our hopes of knowing specific details of the afterlife. However, the contrasts should boost our trust that we will be provided with the Heaven that is right for each of us.

One of the most quoted and beloved descriptions of Heaven for Christians is found in John's Gospel: Jesus says that his Father's house has many mansions. But if we look at the original Greek, mansions had been transliterated into English from *monai*. The Greek dictionary lists "abiding place," "way station," and "place of halt on a journey" as translations for *monai*. The third-century philosopher Origen uses *monai* to describe a resting place on the journey of the soul to God. With this understanding of the text, it could certainly be argued that any number of realities revealed in near-death experiences are indeed mansions in Heaven.[3]

As John H. Hick, the renowned scholar of comparative religions, has pointed out, the Christian view of Heaven, at least in its early sacred texts, is quite open-ended and reticent compared to descriptions suggested by other religions. Heaven is like a mustard seed, or treasure buried in a field. The Muslim Paradise, on the other hand, is described in abundant detail. According to the Qur'an, golden pavilions line the banks of crystalline streams. Some martyrs take the form of emerald birds, safe in their own emerald nests. Others lounge on beautifully manicured lawns and are served figs and plums and wine that never causes hangovers. Sex is available and can be enjoyed guilt free.[4]

But although the details may vary, the dominant and universal attribute of Heaven as reported by religions and experiencers is a feeling of pervasive, all-encompassing love. Every single experiencer interviewed went on at length on the topic. Experiencers tend to become speechless when they talk about the love they felt during their near-death experiences. They repeat themselves, or they use a string of superlatives, or they say all the things it is not, knowing the listener has no idea what he or she is talking about. As Mary Dooley, the fashion designer, said, "This love was different. It was all around me. It was enveloping. It was not the love that a husband or wife feels toward each other, nor was it the love that a mother feels toward her child. It is completely different."

Experiencers try to describe the love they felt with voices filled with awe. Their faces seem lit from the inside with joy and sometimes with tears of longing that they are no longer in the presence of that love. Often their voices trail off into silence when they try to express the power of the feelings. Luckily, sometimes the descriptions of Heaven's love are a bit more articulate. Linda Allan is a soft-spoken woman from Seattle who had a profound near-death experience during a bicycle crash. The narrative itself is richly detailed and profound as far as NDEs go, particularly the way in which love is conveyed to Linda.

After the crash, she lay conscious for a few moments on the ground, but then, she said, "I felt myself being pulled away from myself." She felt frantic. "I knew I was leaving...I knew I wasn't coming back."

Linda describes trying to communicate to her eight-year-old son, to give him information to remember her by, and also to deliver a message to her husband. She scrambled to teach her son in the few moments she had left that he was safe and sound. She had an urgent need to let him know that someone would always be there to take care of him. Then her mood suddenly and dramatically changed.

She floated out of her body. "I was no longer attached to me. I thought that was very odd. I looked down at my body, and it looked awful. I was really glad I wasn't in it, because it was awful lying there. It seemed cumbersome and bulky. Then I was thrown up into the air very, very fast, I would assume at the speed of light, just guessing what that might be, into the blue sky. And it was beautiful up there and it was warm. And when I was floating in the sky, I didn't look at my body. I don't know what I looked like. If I even had a body. I don't know. And then I felt beckoned to my left, somebody wanting me, to have my attention. And I didn't want to look. It was so nice up here. The sky was a blue color that I had never seen before. And it was loving and it was warm.

"But they finally beckoned to me again and I did look over to them again. There were some men sitting there, one sitting closer, but there were four of them. And the first man said, 'It's not your time to go yet.'

"And I thought, 'go where?' I was very innocent and very naive, floating in a sea of air, and I thought it was real odd that he would say that to me. Then they started talking to me with their voices. I was very interested in what they were wearing. They had on Levi's that were kind of worn, the kind farmers or ranchers would wear, and they had on plaid shirts: one green, one blue, one red. And the colors on the shirts—I've tried to explain this to my husband in words, but it's hard—the colors were alive, to please the people who were wearing them and to please me looking at them. Everything there was there to please them and me.

"It was very loving and very happy. The colors would change; all the stripes would change. And if they thought that made me happy, they'd get happier and make prettier colors."

Linda went through a life review with the main Spirit Person, as she called him. After that, as she recalls it, "All these people showed up—hundreds of them, as though they were having a party and they knew me and I knew them, although I don't now. And we were so happy to be there. We had been together before. I knew that. And the Spirit People in the shirts were happy, too. They showed me things beyond that. They showed me, um, I looked over to my right and they opened up something—I don't know what, maybe a black hole—and with all this knowledge that I had they showed me a city. A big city. It had golden colors, and there was this big explosion coming up over the city of lights and rainbows and colors that we don't have here, that we can't even explain. Those colors would hurt our eyes if we looked at them. But not there. It was a glorious, floating, moving city of buildings and a street. The streets had bricks. They were like golden bricks. The buildings next to the street—I know this sounds really strange—but the buildings were smart. They were intelligent. They were buildings of knowledge. I'm not sure what that means."

She did not see any Spirit People in the city. "I was life, the city was life, and I was surrounded with life. And I know that the street went somewhere, but I don't know where. And it's not that I don't know where because I didn't go any farther. I think I don't know where because I wasn't allowed to bring back all the knowledge that I had at the time.

"Then they started talking to me, and I started listening very intently, and I looked at the main Spirit Person who was talking right to me and I was looking intently at his face when it exploded, absolutely exploded, with light and it washed through me, over me, in me, engulfed in this beautiful unconditional love. This person was there for me. I was also there for him, but I didn't know why. And he did this several times. And he just kept exploding with light, and I loved it."

Several sorts of love are expressed in Linda's NDE. There is the forgiveness of love after her life review offered both by herself to herself and by the main Spirit Person. There is the community and friendship of love expressed by the hundreds of people who arrive as though for a party. And there's the love extended by the main Spirit Person with which she was engulfed unconditionally. Of all the attributes of Heaven, experiencers are most sure of love.

In a startling pairing of near-death experiences, the love of Heaven spilled from one experiencer into the life of another. Margaret Lewis Sauro is a chatty and generous-hearted experiencer in her sixties from Rhode Island. Margaret was five years old when she was diagnosed as having scarlet fever. She was put in a hospital for contagious diseases for two weeks before a doctor finally realized Margaret was dying because of a missed diagnosis. He discovered that she actually had a ruptured appendix. Antibiotics had not yet been discovered; she was close to death for several months.

One night, says Margaret, "this marvelous feeling of peace came over me. I was basking in that because it was so beautiful, when suddenly I became aware that someone was holding my right hand. I looked up and my eyes were traveling over a white gown. I came to the head of this beautiful woman. She was wearing like a Roman toga. She had beautiful blond hair, which she pulled back in a chignon, and she had very very fair skin. She had like Roman features, you know, like a Roman nose, very pretty, very slender, and very young. I would place her age from eighteen to twenty-four.

"She walked along with me holding my hand. I kept looking at her. She was so pretty. She did not talk to me or look to the left or the right. She was the epitome of serenity. But then I became aware of a fragrance in the air that was becoming stronger and stronger. It was of flowers, and they just seemed to permeate my whole body. And when I took notice of what was around me besides her, I realized that the path was banked with flowers way over our heads. These flowers were close together the way a Colonial bouquet would be, and they were massive. I was just so overwhelmed by this fragrance that I said to her like a little kid, which I was, 'Are these flowers real?'

"She smiled and looked down at me and said, 'yes they are.' I could see her chuckling, trying to hold back a laugh, because from where I was standing looking up at her, I could see the muscles in her throat working as she was trying to hold that laugh back.

"So anyway, as we walked on several feet I heard faint voices. As we got closer to the end of the path, the voices got a little louder, and I could actually hear what they were saying. One person said to the other, 'but why is she bringing her here?'

'I don't know. She knows better.'

"A few seconds later, at the end of the path, it was very foggy. I could not see who these people were. She took my hand and placed me over to her left, a couple of feet away from them. All of a sudden I became stone deaf. I couldn't hear a thing that they were saying. The next thing I know I was back in my hospital crib.

I looked up and she was standing at the left-hand railing, holding on to it and looking down at me. She said to me, 'I'm sorry, Margaret, but you have to go back now. It's not your time.'"

After that Margaret began to recover. She was in the hospital for almost a year.

If Margaret and Linda Allan compared notes on the geography of Heaven, they would not draw the same map. Linda saw glimpses of a golden city. Margaret learned only of a beautiful arbored path outside a gate. She might conclude that there is a lot of fog, whereas Linda saw none. The similarities are in the loving tone of their experiences. Both Margaret and Linda encountered someone they trusted, someone who was clearly looking out for their needs and guidance.

Margaret tried to tell her mother about her experience, and later a cousin, but they both discounted her account and she learned to be quiet about it. Several years ago, now in her sixties and recuperating from a broken rib, she decided to paint the beautiful lady and the flowers that she had seen. The next day she went to see her internist about her rib, and he brought up near-death experiences. He always asked patients that he resuscitated if anything unusual had happened. Nothing ever had. Margaret took a deep breath and admitted that she herself had had one, that she had just finished a painting of it, and that she would get it reproduced to show him. Her internist had the painting framed and hung it among ten other paintings in his office.

Several weeks later the internist called Margaret on the phone to tell her something strange had happened concerning her picture. A new patient had come to see him for a second opinion. She entered his office before him and stood before the painting as though she were in a trance. The doctor just stood at his desk and observed her, waiting. All of a sudden she turned to him and said, "I know where this is."

He said, "You know what that's a picture of?"

"Of course I do. I walked along that path when I was five years old and almost died."

An experiencer once said that coincidence is God's way of staying anonymous. The second woman, whose name is Mary Olivia Pasterczyk, was suffering from a life-threatening illness so grave that her doctors, including the internist with the painting, were unsure as to whether she should endure treatment or let the disease run its course. She asked the internist if she could possibly meet with Margaret.

In sharing their experiences, Mary Olivia told Margaret that THE MAN (capitalized at her request) as she refers to the Being she walked with along the path, promised her that he would always be with her. Margaret is convinced that God inspired her to paint that place to remind Mary Olivia that God's love is with her.

The trigger for Mary Olivia's walk along the flowered path was overlapping cases of rheumatic fever and scarlet fever. She was five years old. She felt a "release" of herself coming out of her very sick little body. She remembers going through some white, bright clouds. As she says, "It felt good to be out of my body, and I could feel that right away, and I had another body. The clouds were light and full, and they had a depth to them that I just can't find the words to express. It's not just white clouds. There's more to it than that.

"Then I arrived on a path, and I was walking. I met THE MAN. THE MAN and I walked and talked together.

"The place that we walked on was a path, and there were flowers on both sides. The colors were very vivid, not even as you can see colors in this world. They were, like, they were intermingled with me. The colors were just—I don't know—I can't describe it, but they were very vivid, very bright. The sky, if that's what you want to call it, although I don't know that I could call it a sky, but it was in the place that a sky would be, was blue. But I've never seen such a color blue. A wonderful blue." She sighed, remembering. "The colors were just so vivid. They connected with you—they bounced through you. They just were. I have an impression of other vegetation, but I just don't know."

Mary Olivia's descriptions are difficult to read. The stop and start of her sentences, the contradictions and continuous interrupting of herself, come out of the terrible difficulty of putting the ineffable into words. It gets even more perplexing when she tries to describe the feeling for which we use the word *love*. "There was a communication of feelings of love. What a cheap word it has become. I don't like that word. There were communications of something so much greater. Something of that concept was communicated. It *felt* like an open, warm bubble. That sounds so funny to say 'an open warm bubble,' but it was just so warm, accepting, understanding, being with someone who just knew. Knew you inside and out, and outside down. It's like the closest you could ever be to being one with someone. It was a feeling of oneness. I don't have the words!"

Although the feelings might be hard to describe, Mary finds the feelings are still accessible to her decades later. She felt so safe and loved.

"Then it got to a point when he told me I had to go. In my communication with him, I didn't want to. I wanted to stay there. I belonged there. That was home. I didn't want to leave. He let me know that I couldn't stay. I had to go back. He also communicated to me that he would be with me always. He would never leave me. But I could not stay there. I had to go back. I tightened my hand in his. But the next sensation I had was going through the white clouds and entering my very sick little body."

Mary Olivia is a single parent with three children. Her life has not been easy. But even when she was so sick as an adult, she "always had the feeling that things would work out, no matter what decisions I made." She thought it was a "very strange thing" that her experience would be "given back" to her by the painting in the doctor's office. As she says, "It is something I carry with me all the time, but to have it presented to me in that way . . . it was like saying that forty years is nothing. It was just a verification that what he said was true. He would always be with me. I considered myself very lucky."

The painting in the doctor's office was a remarkable coincidence. But was it a message? Of what? Surely the promise in the bower of flowers to Mary Olivia that THE MAN would always be with her would have remained true if she had decided not to endure treatment. So what are we to conclude? That there is a bower of flowers in the kingdom of Heaven? Probably. There may be buildings that are smart and golden trees and an astonishment of colors, too. But the prevailing message of all these near-death experiences is that our souls may travel where our bodies cannot to a Heaven that has many marvelous forms. And the strongest evidence of all is that we can look forward to a Heaven filled with an all-encompassing and accepting love.

NOTES

1. I use this story with Twining's great-nephew's permission.
2. Raymond Moody, *Life after Life.*
3. I am grateful to Tom Harpur, in his book *Life after Death*, for pointing out the importance of looking to the language of origin of sacred texts.
4. For an understanding of Heaven in the Muslim tradition as a place of return to God's love, read William C. Chittick's essay "'Your Sight Today Is Piercing': the Muslim Understanding of Death and Afterlife," in *Death and Afterlife*, by Hiroshi Obayashi.

Chapter 3

Reunion in Heaven: Will We See the People We Love?

Even though I walk through the valley of the shadow of death,
I fear no evil
for thou art with me.

—KING DAVID
PSALM 23:4

Irene Potter, aged ninety-one, was starting the morning at Brightview nursing home with her beloved friend and nurse, Olga. Olga opened the shades and propped Irene up on the pillows. Irene looked up at her and thanked her for all her loving care. She was particularly glad to see Olga, she said, because she was going on a journey.

Irene often made such announcements. She had had a rich and full life and she often "visited" her memories, believing that she was actually going to have tea with a neighbor or go back to her old house in New York. So Olga humored her, as she always did, and asked if maybe she, Olga, could go too. Irene shook her head and said, "Not this time. I'm going to go to my father now. Up and above." Then she quietly died.

Olga happened to look at her watch; therein lies the story. Over the mountain and across town, Irene's daughter Carolyn Wardner, a grandmother herself, was snuggling one of her younger grandchildren in bed. They were "having a little hum-sing" as Carolyn called it, of songs Irene had taught her as a child. Just then, a small carriage clock that Irene had given her when she married began to ring more than a hundred times. The clock had not kept time or chimed in over ten years. It was 8:30 A.M., the time Irene died. As the chiming finally stopped, the phone rang. It was Olga calling to say that Irene was gone.

For Carolyn, who knew the chime mechanism had been broken for more than ten years, the ringing of the clock over and over was a joyful declaration that her mother's soul was communicating to her. She believes that her mother was saying with the means available, "I'm on my way!"

One might suppose that the fact that her mother's spirit, independent of body, gave a final salute to Carolyn would give Carolyn strong hope that reunion would someday be possible.[1] Yet even though Carolyn is a woman of faith who ran a summer religion conference for teenage girls for years and "firmly" believes in Heaven, she is "just not sure" she can hope for a reunion with her mother. During her interview she spoke hesitantly, the ends of her sentences drifting away: "I just don't know if we're really going to see . . . We are so practical, aren't we . . . I'm just not sure about how . . ."

Many people have misgivings about reunion in Heaven. The mystery of Heaven is so much easier to believe in than the specifics. It's hard to imagine, for instance, a cosmic database to organize all the connections between family members. The inclination is to discard the notion of reunion as sentimental.

Sentimental? Surely the longing to see one's deceased mother or favorite cousin or infant daughter is anything but an excess of feeling. Nothing is powerful enough to express the longing to see someone we love whom we have lost to death. Yet in an informal poll on attitudes about reunion with family and friends in Heaven, it was clear that it is a hope wrapped in ambivalence and doubt, even by people of faith. To understand why, we need to take a quick tour of the history of Heaven.

Beliefs about Heaven, like attitudes about food, child rearing, and clothes, go through fashions. Fashions change. In the Christian tradition, Jesus promised the thief dying beside him on the cross that they would meet again in Paradise that very day. Yet medieval mystics, who relied on Augustine for their theology, discounted Heavenly reunions, preferring to concentrate on a beatific relationship with God. Reunion regained fashion in the Renaissance. The intellectuals of the time were entranced with classical Greek descriptions of the Elysian Fields, the land of the dead. Renaissance painters such as Lucas Cranach portrayed the dead cavorting on long lawns around fruit trees, and texts of the time emphasized love among lovers and families in pastoral settings.

This people-based notion of Heaven reached its zenith during the nineteenth century, when Victorian writers waxed poetic about joyous reunions between dying children and dead mothers.[2] It was highly fashionable in Victorian times to believe that the primary satisfaction of Heaven was the reunions with our beloved family members and friends.[3]

In strong reaction to the often cloying notions of the afterlife that the Victorians put forth, twentieth-century notions of Heaven have tended to be fuzzy. The reasons for this retreat into the nondescript are complex and will be addressed in greater detail. But it is important to be aware here that twentieth-century theologians have scorned the descriptions of earlier generations of ministers, scholars, and visionaries. The images of a people-centered Heaven are ridiculed as fantasy or criticized as human constructs that "rob Heaven of its God-centeredness."[4]

As participants in a historical era, we are susceptible to the fashions of the era. The majority of us, for example, think that the nineteenth-century penchant for bustles and hoop skirts is old-fashioned. In the same way, we tend to believe that Victorian notions of lovers separated by death reuniting in ecstatic sexual embrace in Heaven is, well, Victorian. Our queasiness about hope for reunion with loved ones is a reaction to the Victorian mindset.

Although modern theologians may reject the notion of a populated Heaven, modern experience points to a more hopeful reality. Carolyn Wardner feels uneasy about the *concept* of reunion with her mother. But the *experience* of her mother's presence in the ringing bells leads her to trust that reunion is possible. So what is the evidence?

Dying patients often believe they are in the presence of someone who has died. Maggie Callanan, a hospice nurse of great sensitivity, has found that dying patients often straddle two realities. She calls it Nearing Death Awareness. As she says in her book, *Final Gifts,* nearing death awareness often includes visions of spiritual beings or loved ones who have already died, even if the patient's death is not imminent. Dying people may feel warm, peaceful, and loved when they had been feeling great pain or despair; some see a bright light or another place. Callanan points out that many dying patients review their lives and come to a more complete understanding of life's meaning.

The difference between near-death experiences and nearing death awareness is that the process is more gradual for the dying. For days before they die, hospice patients may speak of a light in the distance. They may speak to deceased loved ones for several days or even weeks before death, saying they are not ready to leave yet.

Callanan tells the story[5] of Su, a dignified Chinese woman who was very accepting of her terminal condition. Her husband had died several years earlier. She believed that she could see him standing at the foot of her bed, waiting for her. One day she was agitated when Maggie arrived. Su asked the hospice nurse why her sister had joined her husband at the foot of the bed. Maggie asked Su if her sister was alive. Su said she was, but that she lived in China. Su had not seen her for many years.

The hospice nurse did not try to discredit the vision or solve Su's agitation with medication. Instead, Maggie took Su's daughter, who was there in the room with them, aside and asked her what Su's vision might mean. The daughter replied tearfully that Su's sister had, indeed, died the week before but that the family wanted to protect Su from the news when she herself was so ill. With the hospice nurse's encouragement, the family shared the news. Su's agitation subsided.

Agitation is the key element in this account. Su's personal beliefs of the afterlife are not mentioned, but as a Chinese Buddhist she would have been open to the possibility of visitations from the dead. Chinese Buddhism teaches that souls have mobility; they can travel to sacred mountains that act as way stations on the path of reincarnation. They may also hover in the households of their descendants. Extrapolating from the Victorian model, one might suppose that Su would have lifted her arms in exultant joy at the vision of her sister. The clouds would open, and Su would sink into her pillows in her fevered state and die with a smile gracing her lips. But unlike stereotypes, real life created contradictions. Su was soothed by the vision of her husband and upset by the vision of her sister, hardly the scenario for sentimentality or mere wish-fulfillment. According to Callahan, once Su understood why her sister could be present, she died "at peace and with a sense of anticipation" three weeks later.

A group of hospice nurses was asked at their regular Monday morning meeting if other hospice nurses had had similar experiences. The behaviors Callanan observed in her book were described. The nurses were specifically urged to say if they felt that Callanan had embellished or glamorized the truth. As it turned out, many of the nurses had read *Final Gifts*. When they started hearing the story of Su, almost every nurse began to smile, nodding in confirmation. Most had a similar story to tell. As one hospice nurse said, "We talk about patients having one foot in both worlds."

The hospice nurses have found that the perceived presence of deceased family members is a source of solace for dying patients. One hospice nurse told of a woman dying of throat cancer who was visited daily over several weeks by her twin sister who had died of the same disease two years before. At first, when the dying woman announced in the morning what she had discussed with her sister, the daughter caring for her was rattled. She thought the medications were having undesirable side-effects and complained to the hospice nurse. Over the two weeks before her mother died, however, the daughter came to believe that the conversations had a basis in reality. The sisters were both painters; they discussed favorite paintings and ways to render light. The daughter found that the conversations helped her understand that her mother was comfortable about wherever she was going.

Another hospice nurse described a patient who was severely demented with Alzheimer's disease and who had had several strokes. The patient thought she still lived in the South and talked as though it were several decades earlier. She was unable to recognize family members caring for her or call them by name. The day before she died, however, she regained her ability to talk coherently. She called in her niece to show her the Light that she saw and to describe all the deceased family members who were gathered at the top of the room. She mentioned each family member by his or her name and relationship to her.

Frank Bauer is the only near-death experiencer in this study who saw more than one family member during his brush with death. Frank is a busy man. A retired manufacturing executive, he is now very involved in a service corps of retired executives. Frank was grateful to the Veteran Nurses' Association (VNA) for the superb care they gave his wife, Marjorie, while she was dying of cancer. Frank was devoted to his wife. One of the ways in which he coped with her death was to do fund-raising for the VNA. Several years ago, he himself had a hemorrhaging ulcer. In desperation, he called the VNA. One of the nurses got him into the hospital, where he was in intensive care for six days. A decision was made to operate. During the operation, he had a vision of Heaven.

As Frank remembers his experience, "It was like a beautiful sunset panorama. Up there my mother and dad were just looking at me, but Marjorie was there holding out her hand as if to say, 'Hold it. Take it easy. It is not your time yet.' She had this scowl on her face—the same one she'd have when I used to come out with the wrong tie to match with my suit. The next thing I heard, over to the right, was this voice going, 'Frank, Frank, Frank.' I turned and gave it my attention and opened my eyes. And it was the nurse Sally. She was saying, 'What year is it?' and I said, '1992.' 'Where are you?' 'In Hartford Hospital.' She turned to the doctor and said, 'He's back.' That was my experience."

Frank's father and mother looked about the same as when he'd seen them last. His father had on a business suit and his mother was wearing her winter coat. Marjorie had on a housecoat she often wore. When Frank was asked what he thought was going to happen when he died, his answer was simple: "I'm going to go up and see Marjorie."

George Jehn is an airline pilot and union representative who believes he was reunited with his best friend, during a near-death experience. The day of his NDE, he saw his children off to school in upstate New York, went to a union meeting, and then hopped a plane to Miami to go to a retirement dinner of one of his pals in the industry. The party ended late, but George had good friends from Germany who were on business in West Palm Beach. He decided to drive up to see them. Halfway there he fell asleep at the wheel and rammed into a bridge abutment.

He remembers hearing people shout and watching the ambulance pull up. Although he was lying facedown on the floor of the car on the passenger side, he says he watched what happened from a vantage point out of his body and above the car. Two ambulance attendants got out of the ambulance and ran to his car. Looking down through the roof of the car, George mentally winced as one attendant was about to pick up his hand. He thought he should have felt pain, but he didn't. There was no feeling in his body. George was impressed with how gentle the attendant was with his body. The first attendant turned to the other attendant, according to George, and said, 'Ah, leave him. He's dead.'"

The other fellow came over, picked up his hand, and said, "Let's put him in the meat wagon. We might be able to get a pulse."

Everything went white. For a moment George thought he must be looking at the sides of the ambulance, but then he realized he was somewhere altogether different. As he said in a telephone interview: "First the Light was apparent to me, and then what was apparent was the tunnel I was in that was gray and white. But it had none of the things that you associate with something like that. Rather than being cold, it was warm. It was beautiful. I was going to that Light. That's where I was headed. It was just a feeling of total, total love that enveloped me. As I say, I was headed toward the Light, and that's where I wanted to go. It was fantastic.

"In the short period of time that I was there—although I had no concept of time while I was in there—but anyway, before I made it to the Light, the next thing I knew I was standing in front of a guy. He looked at me, I looked at him, and he was a friend of mine."

George's friend Tom has died five years earlier. They had dated two cousins whom they each married. Tom was already bald at twenty-one when they first met, a side effect of the diabetes that would later kill him.

George tells what happened next: "Tom just looked at me and said, 'You've got to go back, George. It's not your time yet.'

"He looked great," said George, becoming choked up. "When Tom was alive, he was bald and he was so thin. And now he had hair. He never had hair when he was here."

George woke up on a respirator, with wires everywhere, but feeling exultant at having seen his good friend.

In *The City of God,* one of the great texts of Christian mysticism, Augustine takes the original assurance of Jesus that not a hair on the head of those who are granted eternal life shall perish, to conclude that at the time of the resurrection, the body will appear in its ideal state. Saint Augustine's thinking is out of fashion currently because he believed in the resurrection of the flesh. But it is worth noting that throughout the literature of near-death studies, deceased loved ones appear healthy and physically whole.

But what if we do not want to see the people we know who have died before us? What if we dread the thought of a reunion after death? A woman named Elizabeth Pitcher had a father who sexually abused her for years. Even worse, in her mind, was that her mother knew of the abuse and did nothing to stop it. As an adult, a friend of hers said that Elizabeth's parents, both deceased, had appeared in the friend's automatic writing—script that appears to the writer to come from a source independent of that writer. They said that they would not be allowed into the Light until their abused daughter forgave them. Her reaction? That it would be a cold day in hell before she forgave them.[6]

Many people in circumstances similar to Elizabeth's choose to deny themselves the hope of an afterlife rather than imagine the prospect of seeing an abusive family member. But some NDEs offer a remarkable resolution to this conundrum.

When Diana Wood (her name is changed for her protection) was in her twenties, she and her older brother began to fight at a family reunion. The fight escalated into a physical assault by her brother, who crushed her face badly. She had to have more than seven hours of surgery under general anesthesia to reconstruct her features. After several days in the hospital, she was sent home to her parents' house. According to Diana, her family was not outraged by what had happened, nor did they condemn her brother for the harm he had caused her. Diana sank into a deep depression. In her words, she was "willing herself to die."[7]

Over and over she repeated, "I want to die. I want to die."

Suddenly Diana was aware of an altered reality. She heard tinkling chimes that sounded similar to glass wind chimes. She wanted to follow. The tinkling was like a language. Diana found herself asking telepathically who was talking. She was aware of twinkling lights "sprinkled around," which now gathered into a little group. They said that they had something to say to her. If she could reach them, they would give her information to help her want to live.

Diana became aware of a silver cord coming out of her navel stretching like a spider weaving from her to the twinkling lights.[8] She was going to have to use the cord as a tightrope to get to the lights. The lights were very encouraging. She got across. The lights there seemed to be in groups that clustered together, as though they had an affinity for one another.

Diana said, "When I came out there, and was greeted, they said, 'Well, look who's here,' as if I had been there before, as if I belonged to them."

She was told by the lights that the assault was unfair, but that life was unfair, and that she was being given this experience to compensate for the assault.

She sensed that there were clusters of other groups in the distance. The lights explained that she had a core cluster that was not necessarily family. As she tells it, "I felt a closer connection to those people, or those spirits, or those lights that I was with during my near-death experience than I do with my particular family."

As Diana understands what she learned, her connections to her family will be like the concentric circles made by a pebble in a lake. Her father may be in a cluster of lights in the distance, her mother in another cluster. According to what Diana learned, we gather in life because we have something in common that we have to live out. That destiny may be fulfilled by the time we die.

Diana then went through a long life review with the twinkling lights and was taught what she calls universal truths by a Great Being. When she was with the Great Being, he told her that some of her family members are not in her Heavenly circle. He was trying to ease the pain that she felt about the lack of closeness in her family and the betrayal she felt about her family's reaction to the assault.

She asked a lot of questions about life. According to her, the Great Being said, "This time around you didn't get a benevolent and loving family. Your heart is broken because your brother has not been a brother to you. There is evil in the world, too. But you will have another person who will be like a brother to you."

She was told that she would have to make her group of friends her family, and they would love her more and do more for her than her family. He told her that her expectations had been too high for her family.

The Great Being showed Diana different scenes of grieving and joy on earth and explained that life on earth is a lesson. One's job in life is to become a better and better spirit.

The Great Being told her it was time to go, and that he was going to leave her. Diana did not want to go back. The twinkling lights told her she had to return because even though it was several days after surgery, her doctor might take responsibility for her death. It was not in her doctor's destiny to lose a patient. He was a dental surgeon on call who did an amazing job under emergency conditions with hardly any scarring to her face.

The Great Being told her once more that he was going to let her go. Then he vanished. She was out in space, all alone, and it was getting colder. The twinkly stars had also disappeared.

Diana was fascinated with her view of the universe. Again she heard His voice from a distance telling her to hurry. It was getting colder and colder. Diana dawdled. She describes herself as acting like a kid coming home from school looking at the flowers.

The Great Being came back from a distance and said with a very authoritarian voice, "Get back now."

Diana became frightened: "It became so cold that I had to go back. And then *fwump* [sic] I was back in my body."

Diana's near-death experience gave her a perspective that helped her find the will to live. Today she has minimal contact with the hurtful members of her family, and concentrates instead on the sister she feels close to and friends who have become her substitute family. The lessons of the NDE equipped her for life as she needed to live it during this life.

Diana's experience also has implications about relationships in the afterlife. Diana was shown that hurtful family members would be much farther away from her than the loving friends of her immediate cluster of lights. It would seem, by inference, that the painful relationships that we struggle with in this life will not be such a trouble in the next. And the more love that has been created in this life, the more connected to loved ones we will be in the next.

Jesus of Nazareth publicly debated this issue with the Sadducees, a group from the wealthy priestly class of Jesus' time. They asked Jesus who a woman would be married to in the afterlife if she had been married one after another to seven brothers. Anyone listening to the debate during that era would have known that the question was both a trick and a joke. The Sadducees did not believe in the afterlife. They were making fun of apocalyptic believers who thought that when the end of time came, people in the afterlife would be blissfully married and have more children. The apocalyptic believers thought that Heaven would be an extension of life on earth, just happier.

Jesus surprised his listeners by taking neither the Sadducean nor apocalyptic side. A believer in the apocalypse himself, he affirmed belief in the afterlife, but he said that the laws of earth did not apply. Our relationships in Heaven would not be physical but "equal to angels" as children of God. In the context of the rest of Christ's teachings, this parable implies that we will interact in Heaven on the basis of love, not law.[9]

Laurelynn Martin is an experiencer who came away from a reunion during her NDE convinced that the love we give away in this life is the only thing we take with us into the next. Laurelynn was a senior in college on a tennis scholarship, a highly trained athlete who was on her way to a career in professional tennis. She was in the hospital for minor surgery, a twenty-minute procedure called a laparoscopy, when the doctor exerted more than normal pressure and ended up puncturing her abdominal aorta, the right iliac artery, and the inferior vena cava. No blood was getting to her heart or leaving her heart. The needle hit her bowels in a couple of places and went all the way through and hit her spine. She lost three-quarters of her blood.

During this medical catastrophe she had a near-death experience. She tells what happened: "I was up in the upper right-hand side of the room watching, although I didn't connect that it was my body. I just saw this body with lots of red and lots of people running around. I couldn't understand what all the fuss was about because I was feeling great. It was so peaceful and quiet up where I was, and calm. In fact I tried to get their attention to tell them that everything was great. But I couldn't communicate with them, so I went to what I call the next realm of the experience.

"It was almost like coming up through the fog to this darkness. It was peaceful and quiet—the quiet was really important—and it was dark. But the dark wasn't scary. It was all these feelings of peace and bliss and unconditional love and no judgment and absolutely no pain. It was great. And in the distance I saw this Light, and I was going to the Light and the Light was coming toward me."

In the middle of the darkness, before she reached the Light, Laurelynn was greeted by her brother-in-law. She describes him as being at her right upper side. He did not have a physical form. She could not see him. She knew him by his sense of humor, his laughter, and his ability to communicate. Laurelynn says, "It was as though all the things we used to hide were stripped away and he was just this energy form. We were with each other with the core of our being. It was wonderful being with him."

Laurelynn's brother-in-law had died seven months earlier from cancer, when he was thirty-one and she was twenty-one: "It was a great reunion to be with him again. The last time I had seen him before his death I was into my tennis, and into not really paying attention to people. More about paying attention to myself. I had felt bad about that because he had died and I never had a chance to really talk to him."

Her guilt dissolved when he greeted her. "I didn't feel bad about it anymore because he was there with all this kindness and forgiveness and love. So we had a conversation, not with words, but telepathically. What I understood at that time, how it was communicated to me was, 'It is not your time yet. Go back. There has been a mistake.' I look a lot differently at mistakes now, but at that point in my life it seemed simple: there's been a mistake and you have to go back.

"I kept saying, 'I don't want to go back. It's great up here.'

"And he said, 'You have to go back and live your life's purpose.'

"And with that I remember thinking, 'I know how I can get back here and become one with the Light again.' But before I could even voice what I was thinking, because of course everything is known there anyway, so it wasn't as if I had anything to hide, he said, 'No. Suicide is not the answer.'

"That was my message. At least for me," says Laurelynn now. "And I'm really glad I had that message. Because going through my surgical trials and tribulations, it has been really important to know that there is a purpose and reason to get through it.

"We communicated about a lot of things, a lot of knowing of the universe. His last thought was 'Tell your sister I'm fine,' and with that I was dropping back through the blackness. It wasn't scary or anything, but I definitely knew when I was back. I slammed into my body."

Laurelynn has had five major operations and seven years of physical rehabilitation since the botched procedure. She had to sacrifice her hopes for a career in professional tennis. She suffers from hypertrophic scarring, which causes adhesions to crop up inside her body. The adhesions cause debilitating physical conditions. At the time of her first interview, she had just called her surgeon to say that adhesions were compromising kidney function.

Laurelynn has not let her physical disabilities or the smashing of her professional dreams deter her from enjoying a full life. She earned a master's degree during those tough, recuperative years and established a private practice as a physical therapist. Laurelynn was interviewed the week before her marriage. She was looking forward to a wedding trip in Hawaii. Yet she still grieves about coming back from her NDE. As she says, "I would really welcome death. I've had to work really hard to stay here and live my humanness and be in my body. It feels good to be here. But there's always that little bit of grieving for wanting to go back home."

Laurelynn is held here by the message from her brother-in-law that suicide was not a solution, and by the lessons she learned from him during her experience. Far from being a Victorian rapture, Laurelynn's reunion involved hard truths concerning her future that have sometimes run counter to her wishes. She has been tempted by suicide in physically difficult times, but she has not succumbed. Laurelynn believes she learned that her purpose is to spread love and to approach people nonjudgmentally, with total acceptance for who they are. Everything is part of a divine plan. As she says, "The big thing is always to seek knowledge and to love one another. That's the greatest thing of all. The only thing we take with us is the love we have given away."

Unlike the Victorian visions of ecstatic family reunions that have turned even people of faith in modern times against hope of reunion, the reunions of death-related visions have nothing sentimental about them. Quite the opposite. They are simple and quite surprising moments of connection. Hardly rapturous, the hope for reunion touches the grieving, needy place in us all—that place where we have wondered how to keep on living now that a loved one is gone.

Nearing death awareness and near-death experiences in which experiencers have reunions with deceased loved ones are brimming with hope. Laurelynn was allowed to resolve unfinished business and let her sister know that the husband she lost too young was fine. George saw his dear friend healed. Anne can take solace in her knowledge that someday she will join her brother Henry and sister Nora. Anyone who has ever yearned to see a beloved person just one more time should be consoled. The evidence indicates that we will.

NOTES

1. Several other circumstances surrounding Irene's death have entered the family lore. Irene's night-light had flickered all night, and the current went off in her room the morning she died. A family pepper plant burst into bloom that morning. At Irene's graveside, a bird in the tallest tree sang so loudly and insistently that the service came to a stop to listen. "Of course the clock was the most uncanny," says her daughter Carolyn. "It put a different slant on things. There she was, taking flight, saying 'I'm off on my journey.'"

2. A classic example of this genre is *The Gates Ajar*, by Elizabeth Stuart Phelps. A best-seller at the end of the nineteenth century—outsold at the time only by *Uncle Tom's Cabin*—it promised that human love continued in Heaven.

3. *Heaven: A History*, by Colleen McDannell and Bernhard Lang, has a detailed history of Victorian notions of reunion; and *Images of Afterlife*, by Geddes MacGregor, proposes arguments for hope on this score.

4. *Heaven: A History*, p. 308.

5. This account is based on Callanan's lecture at the 1993 annual conference of the International Association of Near-Death Studies, in which the figures appear at the end of the bed. It is not clear in the book account. Her book is titled *Final Gifts*.

6. Elizabeth did, in fact, later forgive her parents, but that is another story.

7. Diane's condition—a postoperative suicidal depression—is less dramatic than most of the near-death experiences used in this book. I have included it because her experience was such a profound one and the aftereffects were so persuasive.

8. A silver cord as a means to pass over to the afterlife is found in a folk Muslim tradition, and also in Ecclesiastes.

9. Luke 20:27–40, Mark 12:18–27, Matthew 22:23–33.

Chapter 4

Can You Get to Heaven
If You've Been Bad?

The quality of mercy is not strain'd
It droppeth as the gentle rain from heaven
Upon the place beneath

—WILLIAM SHAKESPEARE
THE MERCHANT OF VENICE

W.C. Fields, the famous comedian, was well known for his atheism. There is a story, perhaps apocryphal, that when Fields was on his deathbed, his son found him leafing through the Bible. Amazed, the son asked Fields if he was suddenly becoming religious in his old age.

"Hell no," answered Fields, "I'm looking for the loopholes."

Fields's honesty is appealing. He was acknowledging that, in the face of death, even an avowed nonbeliever like himself will entertain faith. He knew that he had been bad during his lifetime. He did not hide from that reality or make excuses for himself. Scrambling for the Bible was a religious act in the most essential sense. The word *religious* comes from the Latin *religare:* to tie back. Fields was indeed tying back to God in the only way he could think of at a critical time. His actions implied that God calls the shots, and that the Bible holds the rules of the game. While Fields would object noisily, I believe he lived up to Saint Augustine's wonderful injunction "to love God and sin bravely."

Most of us are not as forthright as Fields. But, like him, we have probably all looked for the loopholes, hoping that we are not accountable for our wrongdoings. An alcoholic who drank herself to death used to say that drinking made her feel confident—and anesthetized her pain. The child stealing candy says, "But I wanted it so much." The adulterer says, "But my marriage was loveless." The embezzler says, "But I worked so hard, I deserved this money." We all have excuses that we use to reassure ourselves that our wrongdoings aren't severe enough to damn us.

Organized religions respond to the need for loopholes. There was a strong tradition in Christianity and Judaism during Shakespeare's time that as long as you had a good death, you did not have to worry too much about how you had lived your life. When Hamlet was trying to decide when to kill his uncle, he reasoned that the murder must be carried out while his uncle was engaged in wrongdoing so his spirit would go to hell. If his uncle were praying at the time of his death, no matter how dreadful a life he had led, Hamlet would run the risk of encountering his victim in Heaven. If such a notion were correct, Hamlet's predicament would be our salvation: just be sure you're praying when you die, and a heavenly eternal life will be guaranteed.

According to Andrew Greeley, the sociologist, novelist, and Catholic priest, Christianity has always provided loopholes. He tells the Catholic folktale of Jesus taking a tour of Heaven and being aghast at what a motley crew he found there. He hunted down Saint Peter to ask him why he let people with such question-able records inside the Heavenly Gates. Peter swore that he refused each of them entrance. They all went around to the back door, and Mary let them in.

A folk tradition of Islam provides another appealing loophole. When a Muslim dies, he or she has to cross a bridge to get to Heaven. The bridge starts out wide and narrows down to a razor-sharp edge. The less-than-pure will lose their balance, which means falling into hell below. But lo and behold, tradition has it that God designated Muhammad to recover those of us who fall who repent their misdeeds. All you have to do is say "I'm sorry."[1]

Fear of hell is the backdrop of these stories. Whatever our religious training, most of us grew up aware of the moral cliché that you go to Heaven if you're good and hell if you're bad. This assumption is out of favor, currently. Whereas 78 percent of all Americans believe in Heaven, only 28 percent say they believe in hell. A paltry few, and arguably brave, 4 percent of those who believe there is a hell think there is any chance they'll go there.[2]

Hell faded for Jews around the time of Job, and even the most conservative Muslims believe that the longest stay is shorter than eternity. Hell began to cool off for liberal Protestants in the nineteenth century when Calvinism's stern God began to fade. For Catholics, eternal damnation lost its sizzle with Vatican II. "Hell" is not mentioned even once in the hundreds of documents generated.

Modern Christian theologians tend to dismiss hell. They make grand statements about God's love being stronger than any sin a person can commit. They argue that God could not be so cruel as to condemn a person to eternal damnation. Whatever their thinking, scholars do not seem to think it is a subject worthy of their time. When Martin Marty, arguably the preeminent church historian in America, set out to prepare a Harvard lecture on the disappearance of hell, he looked through several indices of scholarly journals, one of which dated back to 1889. He could not find a single entry about hell. A recent book on the subject, *The History of Hell*, by Alice K. Turner, declares in the introduction that the book explores the geography, not the theology, of hell. Turner confides that if she believed in hell, she would never attempt to write about it.

Instead of addressing the possibility of hell, theologians speak of choosing levels of intimacy or alienation from God depending on how we live our lives. One of the most persuasive views has been put forth by Bishop John A. T. Robinson, author of the influential book *Honest to God*. He believes that we all go to be with God. For some of us that will be Heaven; for some of us that will be hell. Robinson believes that if we have developed character and spirit by the way we live our lives that prepare us to be in the presence of holiness, then to be in the presence of a loving God will be joyful. If we have not, then to be in God's presence will be painful. It's a matter of unsuitable companionship. God's presence, for example, may feel a good deal more comfortable for Eleanor Roosevelt than for Adolf Hitler.

The question of hell begs the issue of the hellish near-death experience. Have there been any reports of near-death experiences that were not blissful? The answer is yes.

Marilyn Lawson is a painter and an art teacher. She is a warm, straightforward person who gives the impression that good news is just around the corner. She was only nine years old when she had a near-death experience that swung from the frightening to the sublime. Her burst appendix developed into a gangrenous peritonitis. Emergency surgery was performed. According to Marilyn's parents, the surgeon wanted to give up midway through the operation because he thought the situation was hopeless. Antibiotics had not yet been invented. The surgeon told Marilyn's parents that she would not make it through the night.

Marilyn woke up in the middle of the night in a hospital crib. She describes herself as "in and out of it." Her near-death experience started with the blue light in the hall getting darker. She noticed that the darkness had an existence to it like fog.

The dark, foglike substance filled the room. It seemed to have weight. Says Marilyn, "I found it very hard to breathe. It was like a weight on my chest. The pressure on me multiplied."

Marilyn felt herself sinking. "It was," she says, "as though my bed, with me in it, were going right down through the floor. I couldn't breathe, and I felt like I was going down in this black place.

"The deeper I got into it, the more I realized I couldn't get out myself, and I couldn't breathe. It was real scary. When I was down at a certain level, very low, I couldn't see anything. It was all black and I thought, 'I'm not going to be able to get out of here.'

"Just then, somebody's hand was on my right shoulder. A voice in my ear said, 'Don't worry. Everything will be all right.' The instant those words came in my ear, it was amazing. The weight was gone immediately. I floated up out of the blackness back into the room. I had my eyes open. The whole room was filled with a soft, pink light. There weren't any shadows. Everything was surrounded by this light. And there was a feeling in this light. You could call it euphoria. A real happy feeling. And I thought I have to turn around and see who that was that did that. I looked around and there wasn't anybody there. It felt like someone had come right in through the back of the bed, which was impossible because the wall was there."

Her parents saw her looking around. She remembers her father wondering what she was looking at. When she realized no one was there, she was really disappointed. She rested awhile. Then her frightening descent happened a second time: "The blackness came in the same way. This time I felt mad about it."

Marilyn laughed, remembering. "And I was mad at the guy who said everything was going to be all right. He had a nerve telling me that, and here I'm going down again. I got right down to the bottom, like being down at the bottom of a well or a shaft. It's like I gave up. I remember my thought was 'I bet there isn't any God after all.'

"The minute that thought came into my mind, it was just like someone had reached down with a big fist and grabbed me by the front of my gown and yanked me right out of bed so fast I gasped. It was almost as though He had a furious love: 'I'm going to save you whether you want me to or not.' I opened my eyes, and there was a big thunderstorm going on." (Years later Marilyn confirmed through newspaper accounts that a major thunderstorm was raging that night.)

"'Wow, God's going to get me for this,'" I thought at the time. 'He's mad.' So I'm looking up at the ceiling, and I realized the ceiling is dissolving in the center. I can see right up through it. I can see dark sky and I can see stars. The next thing I know I'm going up through that, higher and higher. I could look down through that into the hospital.

"Through the opening I could see this little person lying on the bed. I wasn't scared or anything: it was oh yeah, that's me down there. Ho hum. I traveled way out someplace in space. It was black sky and stars all around. I stopped there. It was just like someone put their arm around me and held me there, so I wouldn't fall or be afraid or anything."

When Marilyn was asked who was holding her, she said, "I would say God. I can't tell who else it would be. I couldn't see who it could be. I could just feel this tremendous Presence, of love and strength and power, and complete intelligence. Thoughts were going directly into my mind without having to go through my ears, or reading it or anything.

"Then this amazing what I call instant information came into my mind, that God had created all that I could see. Everything. It was like I was part of it and it was part of me. I had this tremendous feeling of relationship with all parts of it. The whole thing was just so tremendous. After I realized that, I gradually floated down into the room. The ceiling closed back up. The room became completely normal, and that was the end of the whole thing."

Marilyn feels that sinking helplessly into the frightening, dark side of the experience occurred to teach her to choose the Light, although she admitted in the next breath that she cannot imagine not choosing the Light. Marilyn did not have a crisis of conscience after her near-death experience. She did not wonder what, in all her nine years of being alive, she had done to deserve the frightening part of her near-death experience. She simply accepted the dark side as a part of God's teaching. When asked if she is afraid of having a similar experience when she dies, Marilyn doubted that she would be scared the next time around. She hopes that she would simply trust that God was with her, teaching her.

Marilyn's reaction to the frightening aspect of her near-death experience echoes the reaction of all sorts of pilgrims and saints who have reported descending into hell. The famous sixteenth-century mystic, Saint Teresa of Avila, was certain that her horrifying out-of-body descent into hell was a purification process. In the Christian tradition generally, journeys into the "dark night of the soul," as Saint John of the Cross called them, are *de rigueur* for anyone aspiring to mystical greatness. Buddhist bodhisattvas who descend to hell to save sinners improve their own spiritual report cards.[3]

What religions throughout the world have always incorporated into their traditions, contemporary near-death research has only recently acknowledged. Frightening experiences are rare in the near-death literature. We need to wonder why.

In *Otherworld Journeys,* Carol Zaleski, a professor of religion and Biblical literature at Smith College, points out that experiencers in the Middle Ages were much more apt to have two stages to their journey, one hellish, one blissful. Experiencers rose out of their bodies to be given tours of scenes of torment. Sometimes demons clawed at their clothing. Sometimes difficult terrain needed navigating. The bulk of the experience was taken up with their being shown their faults and the fate of those who disregard warning. Only then did they ascend to a brief, blissful experience.

So why don't contemporary near-death experiences follow the same pattern? It may be that a message of forgiveness and unconditional love is the message needed in our time. As a source of contemporary revelation, near-death experiencers receive the message we most need to hear. But there are other, darker reasons, too, why frightening experiences do not get the same exposure as blissful ones.

Experiencers are reluctant to come forth with their frightening near-death experiences for fear that they will be judged as deserving a hellish variety. At a meeting of experiencers, a hospice nurse was describing the hellish near-death experience of one of her patients. The patient was convinced that spiders and snakes were crawling the walls and him, and that black hands were grabbing for him to take him to hell. The implications deeply troubled the hospice nurse. She had come to the meeting for feedback.

"Well, if you want to know what I think," answered an experiencer primly, "I think frightening experiences are payback for things done in past lives."

Such reactions should be condemned as casual speculation. We are so quick in this culture to blame the victim. It could just as well be that it takes a person of unusually strong character to endure, remember, and admit to a frightening near-death experience. There is plenty of evidence in literature, myth, and the mystical experiences of saints that only the truly heroic can descend into the underworld and bring back the treasure—in whatever symbolic form—of insight. Until we know more about frightening near-death experiences, we must not judge the messengers.

There are other reasons why not much is heard about frightening experiences. We live in a society so obsessed with feeling good, and so anxious to excuse guilt, that the idea that there might be difficult consequences for wrongdoing is unacceptable. In such a context it is possible that experiencers repress the difficult parts of their experience. Several experiencers admitted during interviews that there was a frightening part that they don't remember.

It may be, too, that researchers, driven by their own hopes and anxieties, only want to hear about the blissful experiences. Experiencers, like all of us, intuit how much they can confide. A researcher strenuously disagreed with the experiencer who said frightening experiences were deserved. After the meeting, two people confided in that researcher that they had had frightening experiences. One had never admitted to such an experience before.

Any experiencer who has the courage to admit to having had a hellish experience deserves admiration. Experiencers who are forthcoming about frightening experiences should be applauded, especially those who agree to share their stories in print.

Charlene Groves[4] was living a hell on earth at the time of her near-death experience in 1951. An assailant used a gun and hammer to smash in her skull after raping her. She had the near-death experience when he tried to strangle her. As she tells her experience: "As I felt myself dying, I prayed because I didn't know whether there was a God. I couldn't figure out if there was one or not because there was so much suffering in my life. I prayed that if there is a God, please take me to Heaven instead of hell. And then

I just surrendered. I felt myself dying. I surrendered to whatever was going to happen. To death."

The next thing she knew she was floating face forward, her arms at her side, into black darkness. She reports with surprise in her voice that she wasn't aware that she had died. "I was just conscious suddenly that this is where I was. Not knowing that I had died, or what had happened to me, or what was happening. I seemed centered, not in my body, but in my mind. I was really alert mentally, probably more aware, more conscious, more sharp beyond any experience of daily life. A very, very powerful Force pulled me and sucked me like an aspirator through the darkness. I couldn't see it, I couldn't see anyone, and I couldn't fight it. It was like magnetized and pulling me toward it. It was like I had no will against it.

"Then I heard low, groaning, scary voices and sounds. I had a feeling there were people just down below me and I was being pulled toward them. Then my heart—I was where my emotions went—my heart was filled with fear, and I panicked. It was more panic than when I was dying. I was afraid that this Power, which I couldn't see, was going to pull me into this horrible-sounding thing. But just when I thought it would, I could feel myself being pulled upward a little bit. It was so scary and so black I thought I was literally just going to [loss for words] blow up.

"Then the blackness changed to gray. And I saw that I was in some kind of very dark tunnel. As I looked around and ahead, I could see rough seams circling around that were lining the tunnel. I was filled with terror as this Thing pulled me. I was just helpless. I was deathly afraid of this seam, for some reason. When I reached that point, the terror vanished instantly. This peace that they talk about in the Bible, the peace that passes all understanding? It filled me. My soul, my emotions."

As Charlene continued to recount her experience, she talked

in terms of "we" traveling through the different stages. "We" is something she alternately calls the "Force," "this Power," "this Thing," the "Energy."

"From then on, we kept going along. The darkness grew lighter as I seemed to go down the tunnel. Then as I got a little bit nearer, way at the upward end of the tunnel, there was a white light. And then the Energy just shot me toward the light. And I broke through into the universe."

Charlene described the universe with a laugh, as though it were both delightful and hilarious to think that it could be described in words. She remembers it as some place high, endless, and vast: "It's not like the sun, moon, and sky, and the planets floating around. There's color there. There's peace. And there's some kind of order."

All Charlene's life she had struggled to understand the meaning of her suffering—not just the rape and apparent murder she was at that time enduring, but a difficult childhood too. During her near-death experience, all struggle for understanding subsided. She was at peace.

"I felt that this was my first spiritual experience," says Charlene now. "I felt surrounded by Spirit. I can't put it into words other than it was a feeling or an energy, an atmosphere outside of my self, and I *felt* it. I felt it emotionally, but I was also aware of Spirit, which had vibration. It wasn't a person.

"After being there for a little while, I became aware that I was completely alone and there wasn't anyone there, no one to communicate with. I still didn't know I had died. I wondered what was going to happen. I felt myself desiring that someone would come. Then something did happen. A huge jolt, a huge force, like a shock, shot me into my body. I woke, and the killer was still beside me. Then my fear returned.

"I can tell you it was terrible to come back and be right where you were before you left. He [the kidnapper] was smoking some cigarettes when I came back. I don't know how many he had smoked. And then he started to conduct the terror all over again. But he didn't strangle me again. I got away."

Charlene believes that parts of her near-death experience were hellish, but that she did not go down to hell. She feels that her experience taught her that there are realms of existence in the afterlife: "You ask me if we all go to the same place. I don't think so. I think we go to someplace that our actions have prepared us for while we were here. There is something like mercy. But I do think there are realms. When I went to that higher realm where the peace was, the grasping, clutching, attacking kind of emotion was not there."

Charlene's near-death experience indicates that there are different realms, and that some are quite terrifying. Charlene's NDE did not create a crisis of conscience for her. Like Marilyn, she did not sit around wondering what she had done to deserve the hellish part of her experience, nor did she make any vows to change her ways. Instead, Charlene's NDE acted as an invitation to a spiritual journey. As Charlene says, "It sent me on, year after year, seeking and reading about religion and the spiritual life. My search brought happiness into my life. Moments of real heightened pleasure and joy and awe."

The question that begs asking, of course, is whether or not hellish experiences indicate that there is a hell. On the basis of near-death experiences, there simply are not enough of them to draw any conclusions. Dr. Bruce Greyson, head of Psychiatry at the University of Connecticut, and Nancy Evans Bush, president of the International Association of Near-Death Studies, have done the only systematic study of frightening near-death experiences.[5] They found that there seem to be several kinds of frightening experiences. One variety catapults the experiencer into an empty void. Some experiences echo blissful ones, but the experiencers perceive them as unpleasant. Other NDEs flip from the frightening into the blissful, as Marilyn's did. Still others contain archetypal hellish material, similar to Charlene's.

As Greyson and Bush are careful to point out, their study must be called preliminary. Over nine years, they were able to cull only fifty experiences from the thousands to which they had access.[6] As Bush has pointed out elsewhere, no one wants to know about or speak up about near-death experiences that indicate cosmic terror. Until more is known, Charlene's sense that there are many "realms of experience" is hard to rebut.

Marilyn's and Charlene's experiences suggest that some realms are better than others, which opens a whole new set of questions. All through Christian history theologians and laypeople have puzzled about what each of us needs to enter the Kingdom of Heaven. Will entrance be the gift of God, through grace, or the result of our own personal effort and good works? The great split between Protestants and Catholics during the Reformation turned on this question. In Hindu thought this dilemma is resolved by a combination of both. Everything depends on the grace of God, call Brahman, whether or not an individual will be liberated from the cycle of rebirth. But all will depend on how an individual uses his or her free will to receive this grace.

Hindus illustrate this theory by describing the way kittens and monkeys are carried by their mothers. The kitten is utterly passive as she is held by her neck fur by the mother cat, a symbol that God's grace is a gift. A monkey mother also carries her baby, but the baby monkey must hold on for dear life. The mother monkey is responsible for the baby's safety and well-being, but the baby must put in some effort too. The evidence from near-death experiences is that monkey babies have the right idea.

Near-death experiences strongly suggest that we are accountable in the afterlife for how we have lived our lives. Many experiencers go through what is commonly called a life review. Experiencers describe having their life presented instantly or as a speeded-up video, or even, for the technologically advanced, as a hologram. Sometimes they are asked essential questions by Beings of Light—questions such as What have you done to benefit the human race? or What have you learned about love? Sometimes they experience how their actions felt to those who were the recipients of them.

Most of us would find the notion of feeling the impact of every one of our past actions perfectly dreadful. It isn't just the really terrible things that we barely admit to. Life reviews seem to include all the little cheaty things too, the million ways we were mean to brothers and sisters, or the way we ignored the lonely kid when we had friends. Some experiencers find they are even accountable for unkind or impure thoughts.

There are some consoling factors, however. Whereas the reviews have lifelong impact on experiencers, the judging process seems to go fast. Albert Heim, who first recorded these life reviews from falling alpine climbers, described the reviews as lives flashing before their eyes. Experiencers say the review goes quickly, and most astoundingly, without crippling remorse. Surrounded by love and compassion and forgiveness, experiencers are asked to view their lives in the context of the love they are experiencing.

At the time of her accident, Linda Allan had married for a second time. Her stepchildren were not happy. Said Linda, "They were very angry. And rightfully so. They worked out a lot of their anger on me and the people around them. I thought it was the most challenging thing I had ever done. I wasn't sure if I could do it, although I wasn't going to give up trying."

Linda's struggle to respond with love to her stepchildren and her efforts to create a blended family with her own son and new husband render Linda's life review all that much more poignant. The review occurred during her encounter with the Spirit People in colorful plaid shirts. As she tells it, "I was watching them, when something exploded from me. A movie. It was all around me. It was three-dimensional and it was my life. Everything I ever thought, felt, said, or did. And everything I ever said to other people, I felt how it felt for those other people. The good things and the bad things. It was instant and it surprised me."

Linda looked at the Spirit People and asked them what was going on. The main Spirit Person seemed very interested in her assessment of her life. As she tells it, "The main person—and I don't know who they are, there was no sign, no one who said, 'I am Jesus,' 'I am God,' there was nothing, but the main shirt person leaned forward and said, 'How was it?'"

"I looked back at him and thought for a minute. For now I was overwhelmed at the knowledge I had. I knew everything about the universe. With all this knowledge that I had, I was able to look at my life from all these points of view I hadn't known before, and make a decision, come to a conclusion. And make a judgment on my life and me."

According to Linda, the *majority* of her life decisions and actions, as she saw them in the review, had been harmful to herself and/or hurtful to others. And yet the Spirit People nodded in agreement when her assessment of her life was positive. Linda said to her judge, "It was good. It wasn't the worst; it wasn't the best. It was good."

Linda then describes the main Spirit Person's reaction: "It was so wonderful when he leaned toward me and looked right in my eyes as if we had just shared a fine dinner and said it was good. As though a decision had been made."

The supportive tone of Linda's life review is so unlike paradigms of judgment we have here on earth. Judge and defendant, employer with employee, teacher with student, even parent with child: all these include an element of power and dominion over the judged. The judge can send the defendant to jail, the employer can withhold a raise. But in the experiencers' life reviews, the goal is not the meting out of fate or punishment but a process for creating self-awareness and honesty. The Spirit Person acted as sounding board and as confirmation, but Linda is the one who made the ultimate assessment of her life.

This sequence of events departs from traditional religious notions of sheep being separated from goats, or some souls departing for Heaven while others descend to hell. Although religion had not been important in Linda's life prior to the NDE, she began to attend a nondenominational church that teaches, from the Bible, that only God can pass judgment. Linda's life review contradicts that teaching because it is Linda herself who passed judgment. When asked about the apparent contradiction with her experience, she said, "Isn't that interesting? I guess something got lost in translation!"

Sometimes the judges need to be persuaded during an experiencer's life review. Steve Miner is a thoughtful young man who reads constantly. He is currently studying at the Lowell School at the Massachusetts Institute of Technology (MIT) for a degree in engineering drawing and is engaged to be married. But life has not always felt so productive and hopeful for Steve. In his mid-twenties he decided to commit suicide out of a profound sense of shame following a fight with a family member.

Steve walked into the water at the beach and inhaled four deep breaths of water to drown himself. He recalls what happened: "All of a sudden my consciousness changed and I went through the range of fear you might expect when you go to die. Then I got to a peaceful place and felt that I heard a rushing noise, kind of like a locomotive.

"I went through a tunnel. As I remember I started to go to the left, and that was an area of darkness and I didn't like the feel, so I started to go to the right. There was light down at the end of the tunnel. I don't remember specifically the thoughts I had in the tunnel except that they were of a questioning spiritual nature. The closer I got to the light, the more beatific I felt. I realized at some point that there was a Being in this light that was communicating with my essence through thought.

"I was judged by some half a dozen judges, who didn't exactly see eye to eye with me. They looked rather like biblical figures with long robes. I explained the reasons why I'd done what I did. The whole time I was viewing them as though I were below and some distance away from them. I remember showing them my perspective. And it was as though space altered a little bit. Instead of seeing them from below, I saw them on an even level. We seemed to see eye to eye.

"I remember wanting to see God. I remember entering into the Light. There was a point that came where the experience became very intense. I remember thinking that if I gazed into the face of God that I would die. So it was a moment of decision. I decided that I wanted to live and try to make a better go of the latter part of my life than I had the first part."

Had Steve's life review alleviated the sense of shame that had motivated his attempt to kill himself? Or had it reinforced that he had done something wrong? He said neither. In fact, evaluating his actions did not seem to be the point at all. As Steve says, "The only thing that mattered was getting at the truth. Every thought, word, and deed that you've had comes into account. I mean that. I felt both accountable and forgiven. The judgment seems to be in part done by yourself. And the forgiveness"—his voice drifted off for a moment— "I mean what I understand to be the presence of God is total light and total love. There is no animosity there. In the presence of those judges I totally bared my soul. And when I was satisfied and they were satisfied that the truth had been told, then we saw eye to eye."

The goal was clarity. As soon as Steve achieved clarity, he moved into the Light and made a decision to return. The goal of the life review was not to arrive at a fair punishment but to attain the clarity needed to move closer to God's love.

The judges act like coaches for truth. Often the judged are doing the actual judging. Once an experiencer is utterly clear, she or he proceeds to the next part of the experience, usually the teaching of universal truths.

In Linda's case, at the moment of closure when the Spirit Person said "It was good," a party began and she was given spiritual knowledge. Whereas Linda's life review seemed to be a stepping stone, Steve's was a defining moment: he decided to return to his life in order to "make a better go of the latter part of my life than I had the first part."

The same process was in play for Diana Wood. In her life review, the twinkling lights all around her took a more assertive role than Steve's judges. First she had a conversation with them to see if she had the strength and clarity of heart to go on to the next step. "Even the smallest thing that you do has an effect," Diana quotes the twinkling lights as telling her.

Diana was shown a scene from her childhood when she was in second grade. It was the first time she had done something deliberately wrong. She switched a broken blue crayon from her crayon box for a better one from another child's box. During the review of her life she would sometimes try to make herself look like a better person than she was. Diana describes it as "fudging the truth." Whenever she did so, however, the twinkling lights would go "*awwwww,*" in a skeptical tone, and she would become more truthful.

When Diana would claim that something wasn't her fault, she

was shown how she played into the relationship. "They were trying to get me clear. They used the expression to see right through
me. I had to pass the test of honesty before I could go to the next
step of the life review. My character was being tested.

"They broadened the experience [of the assault], taking it
away from the personal and saying 'yup, the world is a tough
place,'" explains Diana now. "They were saying 'look what else
happens. So you got your face smashed in. Look what happens
here.' They were testing me to see if I was strong enough to handle my own truth."

According to Diana, she was shown in her life review that she
was not the innocent victim and nice person she thought she was.
"They were pointing out hard truths about myself," says Diana
now. "My pain was going to come from my own pain against myself."

Both Diana and Steve were accountable to judges, although of
different garb. Both believe that the purpose of the life review was
self-awareness and complete honesty. For Steve the process re-
sulted in the lifting of his shame. He now says that he cannot conceive of a situation in which he would attempt suicide. For Diana,
the process lifted her sense of being a victim. In understanding
her own responsibility for how her family interacts, she could face
living with the conflict. In each instance, the experiencer's conscious attitude was altered with the help of the judges.

In Warren Doe's life review, the circumstances seem different
but the message had the same life-changing impact. Warren is a
potter and sculptor who decided to commit suicide in his twenties
because of confusion about sexual identity and problems resulting
from a tour of duty in Vietnam. He filled his small foreign car
with gallons of gasoline and slammed into a bridge abutment
going eighty miles an hour. The guard rail penetrated the car; he
became unconscious when the steering wheel hit him. He went to

what he calls "an in-between place that the Catholics call purgatory."

Born and raised a Baptist, Warren remembers thinking, "'Oh my gosh, the Catholics are right.' Suddenly I was there. I was in this grayish area, with a light above me. When I realized where I was, I saw the Earth and realized that what I had conceived as God—all knowing and omnipotent—that's what I was. Yet I also realized as part of that knowledge that I was part of the Light, part of God in general, like pieces of sand on the beach. I was one piece of sand that was a God, but God itself consisted of the whole beach. I definitely remember thinking that everything made sense. I had all knowledge. I understood why a million people get killed in an earthquake. I understood the total balance of the world, and why it operated the way it did. All my answers were there."

One might suppose that a realization of such magnitude would be exhilarating, but there was a hitch. "I also got frightened for a moment," says Warren. "I didn't know where I was. A person spoke to me, telepathically. I didn't see the person, and then the person took shape. And this person, the only way I can describe it to you, was that this person was a cross between an angel and an attorney. This person basically said, 'I'm going to represent you,' just as in a courtroom here on earth. I understood that my case was going to be considered.

"I cannot tell you that I reviewed my whole life. It seems to me that I was asked to contemplate whether I wanted to go back to earth. And I knew because of my knowledge that existence on earth is one of the most important experiences you can possibly have. The problem was, I didn't know what condition I was in down there. At one point my reasoning was, it doesn't matter what condition I'm in. Because even if I were in a coma, the ability to listen to the nurses coming into the room, making a few jokes, the experience of being there, is reward enough for existence.

"I suddenly had this awareness that to be, even in a vegetative state, is extremely valuable. To breathe. To feel the sensation of breathing. So my answer was right away, 'I want to go back.'"

The angel-attorney asked Warren if he would take his body back. "That was the only moment when I zoomed in on myself from above. I could see right through the car roof. I could see myself lying there in a mangled mess, but I could not feel. It was just a vision of my appearance. I couldn't tell what condition I was in. I said yes."

This decision to go back to his body, even at the risk that it might be a "mangled mess," was made by the same young man who had methodically planned to have the car he was driving explode in flames with him in it.

Upon saying yes, Warren zoomed back into his body. But somewhere just prior to his return, he saw a scale. As he remembers the moment, "I didn't see a courtroom, but I knew that something was happening. There was only one thing in this process that I actually saw from that state out there, and that was a scale. As stupid as it sounds, it was the same kind of scale that you'd see on a court building, a scale of justice."

On the scale, Warren could see little specks that he alternatively describes as dust or tobacco or gold. "Now I always thought that I was a Goody Two–shoes," says Warren. "Prior to this suicide attempt I had spent hours working for society, scouting, all this stuff, tried to be a good person, an honest person. Frankly I really figured the scale would be weighed in my favor."

The reality came as something of a shock to Warren: "The scale was really close. It was *really* close. Oh, gee. But the grains were in my favor, although small. That's one of the reasons I was allowed to return."

Bill Pacht says he did not go through a life review during his NDE. But when his mother, who is dead, walked into the operating room where he was having bypass surgery, he was sure she was going to castigate him for things he feels guilty about. What he learned surprised him. Says Bill, "There are some things I've done that are bad. I remember thinking, 'If I die, my mother is really going to give me a lot of crap for all this stuff.' But when we were communicating, she kind of dismissed all that. None of that matters. It's just the kind of thing humans do. She let me off the hook for a lot of stuff.

"I remember sitting there, and the first time she walked in I remember thinking, 'She's going to yell at me for masturbating, ninety-seven thousand times.' But then she gave me a complete calmness, like that's nothing, nothing. Doing the wrong thing is not bad, because it is part of being human. The thing is to see if you learn from it.

"As she said to me, 'you know, if you cheat on your wife, that's not bad, but it's what you do with it.' Each thing is a test. Like if you cheat on your wife for example. I don't know why I use that example, maybe I shouldn't, but that's the example she gave me. You can get stuck at that level, doing it and doing it and doing it. That's not bad, but you're not going to grow from it. These are all, I don't want to say tests, because I hate the word, but obstacles. I don't like that word either. Benchmarks. They are all something that is the measure of the person, that are given to you in your life."

Flawed human beings go through a life review, feel forgiven, and proceed toward light and love. No Saint Peter pointing up or down, no bridge from which to fall, no Hell or Gehenna or Hades. In symbolic terms, these life reviews indicate that we are accountable. But the purpose of the life review is not to mete out reward or punishment as appropriate. Rather, the purpose seems to be self-knowledge, to become so clear that the experiencer can move closer to his or her true purpose.

Think again of W. C. Fields, hoping that he was not accountable for his wrongdoings. If the judges are on our team, coaching us in self-knowledge so we may come closer to God, his scrambling for the Bible was unnecessary. I can imagine Fields, thoroughly surprised and cracking jokes about Philadelphia, becoming dumb with terror as he is given a tour of the Dark. Surrounded then by love, he reviews the harm he caused, basks in the laughter he created, and moves into the Light.

NOTES

1. The same blessing exists in the Zoroastrian tradition, which is thought to be among the world's oldest living religious traditions. Instead of the bridge of al-Aaraf, it is called the Chinvat Bridge, and the "catchers" are called bodhisattvas, but it is the same loophole.

2. Gallup poll, 1991.

3. Christopher M. Bache covers the idea of NDEs playing the role of purification of the soul in his article on frightening near-death experiences in the *Journal of Near-Death Studies*, 13, no. 1. For more on Saint Teresa, read her autobiography, *The Life of Teresa of Jesus*, trans. E. A. Peers (original work published in 1565).

4. Charlene's name has been changed to protect her. Her assailant may still be at large.

5. Their article, "Distressing Near-Death Experiences," appeared in *Psychiatry* 55(1992): 95–110.

6. This study, too, is based on about the same number of experiencers. But whereas this study is backed up by thousands of experiences and a plethora of other research, Greyson and Bush have found experiencers typically reluctant to share frightening experiences.

Chapter 5

Who Will Guide Us?
Angels, Guides, and
Spirits of Light

*Fear not: for, behold, I bring you good tidings of
great joy.*

—LUKE 2:10

I am borne away by the mighty and shining ones.

—EGYPTIAN BOOK OF THE DEAD

Sarah and Abraham had been married
ten years but had never had children.
Sarah wanted a baby so badly, she offered
her maid to Abraham. The moral value of
monogamy was not yet established; Abraham agreed to the idea. It is not clear if
Hagar, the maid, had a choice.

The Bible does tell Hagar's reaction to
conceiving: she treated her mistress with contempt. Probably younger and more lovely,
probably blessed with smooth olive skin and
crowned with sleek hair, Hagar must have
imagined that her talent for conceiving babies made her the better woman.

Hagar misgauged Sarah when she let

her feelings of contempt show. Sarah stomped off to Abraham and said, "May the wrong done to me be on you."

It is not entirely clear what exactly Sarah was threatening—the withholding of her more experienced sexual favors? No veal or milk and his favorite bread for supper? Whatever. Abraham told Sarah to deal with the problem however she pleased, and it pleased Sarah to deal harshly with Hagar.

So Hagar ran away. An angel caught up with her by a spring of water in the wilderness. Unwed and in a foreign country, Hagar was open to the advice of a stranger. The angel told her he knew she was pregnant. _I know you,_ that angel was saying. _I know your secret and therefore your soul. I'm here with a message to help you._

The angel told Hagar she should go back to Sarah. He promised her that she would have a son who would be powerful. Hagar was amazed, grateful—and humbled by the encounter. She says, in one of the more essential questions ever asked, "Have I really seen God and remained alive after seeing him?"[1]

Hagar's question reveals an attitude of awe quite different from the contemporary stance toward angels. Angels have been in fashion lately. There are angel calendars and angel newsletters. There are angel postcards and angel pins, and New Age music that is called angel music. Pricey catalogs and Christmas shops carry ornate figurines of angels. There are even courses on how to get in touch with your inner angel or your guardian angel.

All this attention, even trendiness, may have clouded the incredible power of angels. Angels are God's messengers. To be in an angel's presence is to be forever changed. The ancients, like Hagar, knew to fall on their faces with amazement after an encounter with one.

In Judges 13 of the Bible, a woman was out in a field when a stranger appeared out of nowhere. He told her that he knew she had no children, but that she would soon bear a son. The woman ran to tell her husband, Manoah, who asked the angel for advice about the pregnancy and then offered the stranger some dinner. The angel turned down food but suggested that an offering be made to God. Manoah asked the stranger his name, in order that they might honor him when the baby was born. The angel replied, "Why do you ask my name? It is too wonderful."

The couple prepared the offering as the stranger requested. As the cereal and lamb burned, the flame from the altar leaped toward Heaven. The stranger ascended the flame. Only then did Manoah and his wife fall on their faces to the ground, knowing that they had been in the presence of the holy. Nine months later, Samson was born.

Living in modern times, we have so many Italian Renaissance paintings, Hollywood images, and Hallmark cards of angels in our visual repertoire that it is easy to forget how simple and powerful angels were in the Judaic-Christian tradition originally. They did not come with wands or halos or wings. They did not announce their significance. They came to Abraham in the midday heat of his tent. They came to Gideon as he was threshing his grain, and to shepherds watching over the flocks. Angelic company had not been expected.

The Guides and Beings of Light of near-death experiences conduct themselves in much the same way. They do not have wings or halos. They do not give their names. They appear, unbidden, to the experiencer to give a message. And although experiencers do not fall on their faces in amazement as the ancients did, they are forever changed.

According to Linda Allan, the Spirit People, as she calls her angelic Guides, returned Linda to her body. She reentered through her thumb and her finger. Says Linda, "It was like a very comfortable, warm wave as I went back into my body. At that moment I was lying there, and my husband picked up my hand. It all happened in one smooth motion. I looked at my hands and they were glowing [like the Spirit People]. I could see through my hands, and they became more solid and glowing. And John [her husband] was glowing, too, which gave me a lot of comfort."

The Spirit People then showed themselves to Linda three times to help her handle the physical pain of her accident after she was back in her body. She was suffering from severe concussion, whiplash, and a dislocated shoulder. As Linda remembers it, "They showed themselves when the pain got too excruciating—as [the orderlies] put me on the stretcher, again in the ambulance, and then again in the hospital when they were giving me a CAT scan."

There is some indication that the technician administering the CAT scan was also aware of the Spirit People's presence. The pain during the CAT scan was significant, either because Linda was so hurt or because she had been handled roughly. As she remembers it, "The Spirit People had come and were laughing and smiling and nodding at me. [They were] saying, 'It's okay to feel pain, but we are always with you. How silly of you ever to doubt us.' I felt comforted.

"That's when the technician came out looking shaken, saying 'I could have sworn there were voices out here. But that couldn't have happened. There's no one in here.'" According to Linda, the technician continued: "I came out twice to check, and I thought it was you, but you don't have a man's voice. And there was more than one man's voice speaking to you. Are you okay?"

Linda could tell the technician was frightened. She did nothing to assuage his fear. As she says now, laughing, "I thought, I'm not telling you anything because you were so rough with me!"

Linda had a rough time adjusting after her near-death experience. By her own description, she would whine on walks at night under the stars. Often she cried, longing for the powerful love she had felt from the Spirit People in Heaven.

"But that almost got to be too much," says Linda now. "I prayed that I could be veiled from that feeling of love and connectedness to Heaven. It was too intense. It replaced the feeling of love and connectedness that I had with my husband. It put him someplace else on my priority list. And I was feeling the loss of that. It made me sad. So I asked them to help me with that. At this time I wanted to have a human physical body that I could wrap myself around, that would wrap himself around me, because I can't touch Heaven while I'm here. I needed love in flesh and bones. And they did! I no longer felt that tremendous loss and yearning for Heaven. I felt connected back to my husband."[2]

Linda's desire to be veiled from the feelings of love and connectedness to Heaven is an unusual moment of religious life. Think of all the yearning, doubting souls through the millennia who have wondered if their faith is justified. Imagine all the theologians, ministers, rabbis, and priests who have preached faith to their congregations and then called on God in the privacy of their own prayers to lift their overwhelming doubt. Perhaps you yourself have asked for just one small sign that God's silence is empathic and not empty. Yet here is a woman of no previous religious background who is so sure of Heaven's love for her that she asked that the metaphoric radio waves connecting her to the Spirit People be turned down.

Other experiencers have also found that once they have encountered an angel—or some other name for holiness made visible or verbal—their encounter gives them an awareness of Presence in their lives after the near-death experience. Linda Burnett believes that her near-death experience taught her that there is no death; those who have departed this life before us continue to be available to us. Says Linda, "There are helpers, spirits, saints, and apostles for help and information. We can access help." She laughed. "Sometimes they turn me down."

Gerri Klynn has been aware of Presence almost all her life;

she had her first NDE when she was three years old. She fell off the landing of the third-floor outdoor staircase all the way to the sidewalk. As she describes what happened, "I remember then, as a little person, watching my mother crying and holding me. And I was in the arms of someone—I would say Jesus—holding me and comforting me. And I said, 'I've got to go back. I can't leave my Mom.'"

That's the entire near-death experience. Dr. Melvin Morse, the leading researcher of children's near-death experiences and author of *Closer to the Light*, points out that children almost always have very short experiences. He speculates that they do not feel the same pressure to create a narrative as adults do.

When asked how she knew it was Jesus, Gerri said it was "just a knowing, a spiritual knowing. It's being safe, it's knowing your father is with you, your real father. I'd have to say that I always thought that it was light. I didn't see a person with a robe on or anything like that."

When Gerri was seventeen, she became pregnant by a man she did not love. Right up until the last moment in the courthouse in Chicago, she did not know whether she should marry him. She looked out at the water of Lake Michigan and said, "Tell me what to do." She heard a voice say no. Twice more she heard the voice say no, but her mother pushed her forward, and she said yes.

Was the voice just her conscience? Was it an angel guide? Gerri does not know. But she says that she knew at the time she would regret not obeying it.

As an adult, Gerri was tobogganing with her family on a very large hill. On a fast run, she flew off the sled and hit her shoulder. She called to her husband. She was in the dark. Gerri thought to herself, "Why am I calling him—he can't help. Call God."

So she did. As she remembers what happened, "Immediately there was this very bright light, which was very scary. When I got to the Light, it was like the air there was so serene. I remember thinking, 'why can't I feel this on earth?' I mean the contentment that you have, it is unexplainable in words. It is just so contentful and serene. It's just bliss.

"I felt that there were two entities, one on either side of me. The grass was very long, and I thought, 'What are we doing here?' The grass is so long, and this is so wonderful, but I belonged back there with (my family). I could see them. The entities were just taking me along. And for just a part of a second, which seems long, I thought, 'I'm going to stay. This is just too good.' I was just going along on the grass with them.

"Then I heard my children's voices and my brother-in-law panicking and I thought, 'I can't do this, I can't leave them.' And I said, 'Take me back.'

"They said, 'Are you sure?'

"I said, 'Yes, please take me back right now.'"

Gerri could hear her children calling to her but was fully present with the entities. Her ability to straddle two realities may be connected to the presence of the entities.[3] She communicated with the entities by mental telepathy. She felt them rather than saw them.

"They said, 'But you're not going to get any help, and you'll be by yourself for a long time.'

"And I said, 'That's okay. Take me back.'"

Gerri interpreted the entities' message to mean that she would not have a lot of people around to be supportive to her. When they asked her if she was sure she wanted to do this, she believed they were telling her that her life was not going to be easy.

"Meanwhile my brother-in-law was coming toward me, and I went back exactly the very same way, through the tunnel, through the dark part ... He was panicking. First he was laughing, and then he was realizing something was terribly wrong with me. So when I came to, they took me to the hospital because my shoulder was so badly hurt."

Gerri's life has borne out the prediction of the entities. She had two more children after her near-death experience, bringing the total to five. She tried to leave her husband several times but had no money and no education. It was seven years before she found the courage to get a divorce. She went back to school and earned her high-school degree, then her secretarial-school degree. She is now studying to be a massage therapist. Along the way, she has worked as a bus driver. It was while driving the bus that she saw the angel.

Gerri's assignment as a bus driver was driving children with special needs. Gerri was especially drawn to one little boy. Knowing that the family was considering placing the child outside their home because of the many difficulties in caring for him, Gerri used to pray for the boy's development. One day as she turned to help him off the bus, there was a huge and radiant angel standing just behind him. According to Gerri, the angel had no gender. "It was gorgeous," says Gerri. "It wore a beautiful white dress and this long golden hair. The light took over the whole bus."

It is worth noting that modern physics can be used to prove that Gerri's vision of an angel at the back of the bus is eminently possible. *Buckaroo Banzai* is an obscure science fiction movie of the eighties that physicists like to cite as an outlandish and entertaining lesson in quantum physics. Banzai is a neurosurgeon who is also a fanatical race-car driver. He does his physics and math, gathers friends, fans, and the military to watch, and proceeds to drive his race car through a mountain without harm. His explanation to the quickly gathered world press? He drove—fast—in the space between the atoms. Mathematically, he can't be proven wrong.

The theological repercussions are endless, however speculative. In the same way Buckaroo drove through the mountain, modern physics can "prove" mathematically that an angel can travel here, and that angels could travel through doors or disappear at will. What cannot be proven or seen is what the angel really is. But the very fact that there is now room for angels is of great religious significance. Angels and Heaven itself in purely mathematical terms may be above us, around us, in the space between our own atoms and toes.

Mary Olivia Pastercyzk does not need the math. She had an encounter with an otherworld Being during a near-death experience that feels as real to her as housework—with the rules changed. As she describes talking with THE MAN, "It wasn't talking as you and I are talking. No words were needed. I don't know, I guess you could say telepathic, but I hate those words—I hate them. We knew each other's thoughts and we communicated that way. He held my hand and we walked. He had a white robe on. Don't ask me why he had a white robe on. I don't know. Because I was a little child, and I only came up to about his hands or wrist area. I remember looking at the folds of this white garment that he had on and I never looked up at his face. I don't know why. It's not that I couldn't have or shouldn't have. There was just no need to do that. Now I think to myself, 'I'm forty-seven years old and I say, why didn't I look up at his face?' But at the time it was no issue.

"Anyway, when I first encountered THE MAN, I came to him with my concerns. They weren't the concerns of a little child—their toys or their mommy and daddy. I don't know why, it's just my personality, I was concerned and communicating for the world, the place that I had just left. Things that were going on there. He let me know that we were very important here, but that was here and this was there."

This sense of otherness, "That was here and this was there" is a message often communicated by guides in near-death experiences. Bill Pacht, for instance, discovered from his deceased mother that none of the issues that had plagued him with guilt mattered on the other side.

Mary Olivia was very aware of the differences between where she was and earth reality. Her description of the telepathic communication between her and her guide is one of the more evocative accounts. She says, "The communication was like a wind that blows in and out of you and you understand everything. And that's just how the communication was. We encompassed everything. But how can you encompass everything and not be specific? I don't know. But that's the way it was."

She continued to be struck by the oddity of her connection to THE MAN. "We walked. It's funny, because the physical sensation of walking was walking, but the communicating was not talking. I don't know why, but I was definitely a body, a different kind of body, but a body. Recognizable, too. Another experience that I had was that while I was doing it, I could see myself doing it. Walking. And talking. It was very dimensional—it wasn't just one dimensional. It contained many, many dimensions.

"I don't know how long I was there, but we did a lot of things, and we covered everything. We walked along. We held hands, which was really very wonderful. I can still remember the imprint of his hand in my hand, probably more than I can remember my dirty kitchen floor, which I've looked at many more times."

Mary Olivia laughed—a long, rollicking sound.

The doctor was there with her mother when she woke up. He told her that she was so very sick that they thought she had died. Says Mary, "I told them I did. They pooh-poohed it.

"I didn't care what they said," says Mary now. "I knew. I still have the feeling that that was much more real than this world is. It's a different reality. It's a totally different place."

Mary Olivia was asked during the interview who THE MAN was. She made it very clear that she wanted to use capital letters, but she resisted speculating about who THE MAN was. "I would never presume to say," she said. "I didn't ask him. I just knew that he was THE MAN. People say to me, 'That was Jesus. That was God.' It may well have been, but that doesn't concern me. I just know it was reality. I, of course, have my own references from what I had learned in this world, but I don't put it on that. I don't want to. It may not necessarily be what we think."

As Carol Zaleski, Ph.D., points out in *Otherworld Journeys*, the medieval mind derived comfort in finding links to the traditional. Connections between biblical angels and death-related visions of guides and Beings of the Light such as THE MAN would have convinced them that the near-death personage is neither new nor incredible—and therefore is believable. The modern mind, on the other hand, tends to look for the unprecedented and the eccentric to verify new phenomena. The implication is that because "this"—which, in this case, is angels—could not have been made up, it is therefore authentic.

Mary Olivia's encounter with THE MAN fulfills both criteria. Like biblical angels, Mary's Guide meets her on the road and does not give his name. He acts with complete authority, which Mary, no matter how much of a tantrum she may have wanted to pull, knew she would obey. And yet there are aspects of Mary's experience that are unprecedented and eccentric, too. There's the fact that she never saw his face, and that she can feel the imprint of his hand on hers forty-two years later. There are the telepathy and the multidimensionality of her perceptions. Also persuasive is her insistence on describing her feelings as a "warm, open bubble" even though she knows such a description does not quite compute. Her commitment to describing the experience as it really was is far greater than her desire to please the interviewer, or make sense in a book. What matters to Mary is THE MAN's promise that he would always be with her.[4]

He would always be with her. The fear of being abandoned is such a primitive one. It comes into high relief when death is confronted. In *A Grief Observed*, C. S. Lewis, the celebrated scholar and storyteller, tells of his mortally ill wife's saying frequently in the months before she died that she felt she was going "alone into the Alone." Even Jesus Christ, who Christians believe is God Incarnate, participated in the terrible aloneness of death: "Why hast thou forsaken me?" he cried out just before he died.

But the promise of most religions is that we will not be alone when we die. In one of the few direct statements Jesus ever made about the afterlife, he turned to the thief hanging on the cross next to him and said, "Truly, I tell you, today you will be with me in Paradise."[5] The Qur'an gives detailed descriptions of the attendants who will serve fruits and other nourishment to the new arrivals in Paradise.

Followers of a branch of Mahayana Buddhism in Tibet believe that those who have died meet deities. One of its sacred texts, *The Tibetan Book of the Dead*, describes an elaborate sequence of events during the forty-nine days after death.[6] To guarantee that the faithful will not be alone, the *Book of the Dead* is read to a dying person as a guide through the *bardo* states between death and rebirth (literally, *bar* "between," and *do* "two"). The intent is to help him or her understand what is happening in death and to give advice on what to do at each stage. The sequence described is compellingly close to that described by near-death experiencers.

In the first *bardo* state, the self separates from the physical body and is surrounded by an intense and blinding light which is called the "Radiance of the Clear Light of Pure Reality" (a great name for what experiencers try to describe). If the self is not ready to enter into the Light, it goes onto the second stage of the *bardo* experience, in which the self meets any number of angel guides. In one particularly evocative translation these are described, among others, as the Peaceful Deities—enveloped in brilliant colored lights—Wrathful Deities, the Doorkeeping Deities, and the Knowledge-Holding Deities. The angels, guides, and Beings of Light described by experiencers all fit into one of these categories.

Great religions promise that we will have company. Death-related visions do, too. Hospice nurses tell story after story of dying patients reaching out with joy to someone unseen just before they die. The near-death experiencers in this book are frequently met by guides, Beings of Light and other angel-like helpers. Warren Doe was met by what he calls his "angel-attorney," who told him that he had made the right decision in returning to earth life. Steve Miner came before a panel of judges and discovered that they "did not see eye to eye" about his life. Mary Free was accompanied through her experience by the Creator and was told wonderful secrets about the unity of the universe. Pat Bryson and Betty Jane Ramsey believe they were greeted by Jesus Christ. Diana Wood was guided by the twinkling lights and the Deeper Voice, as she calls him, who instructed her on the role of suffering. In this chapter alone, there are Spirit People, entities, and THE MAN.

Such angels, entities, and spirit guides reassert God's Presence in our lives through the messages they give. Almost all religions hold that God in His and Her full glory is too much for humans to bear the sight of. Metaphorically, we need pinhole cameras and solar film to protect us from the full radiance of whatever God is. So God gives us the filter of angels. Angels are God made visible and verbal in a form humans can manage.

Does that mean that an angel is the same as God? Of course

not. The word for angel in Greek, the language of the Bible, means messenger. God speaks to us in the language we can understand. In the case of Hagar, for example, a stranger with dusty feet standing at a well spoke a message she could hear and trust.

It has been said that the more a culture dwells on angels, the more remote that culture is from its understanding of God. If that is true, God is lassoing us with a very long rope indeed with all the stories and near-death experiences abounding currently about angels. And however rich and significant each single message is, the power of angels is also collective. They serve to remind us that God's Truth is still unfolding. Muslims believe that Muhammad wrote the received and sacred word of Allah. Christians believe that God's messages are fulfilled in Jesus Christ. Yet both traditions believe, too, in the messages of angels that came after their prophets. The angels, guides and beings of Light in near-death experiences suggest that revelation of Heaven is still possible in the late twentieth century.

No matter what the name, all these representatives of the Unknowable have characteristics in common. They greet and they guide. They deliver God's messages. The angels, guides, and spirits of Light in near-death experiences give reassurance that we are not alone in the universe, at death or any other time.

In a story that has many versions, a guardian angel is conducting a life review with a new arrival in Heaven. For the first time, the soul can see how many times her guardian angel intervened in her behalf. At one point, she sees both their footprints in the sand; later there is only one set of footprints. "You see, it was just as I thought," complained the newly arrived soul bitterly, "in my time of greatest need, you deserted me. There's proof: only one set of footprints."

"That's because I was carrying you," said the guardian angel.

NOTES

1. Genesis 16:13.

2. P. M. H. Atwater has written on the problems of adaption to earthly life after an NDE. To pursue this topic, read her *Coming Back to Life: The Aftereffects of the Near-Death Experience.*

3. The only other experiencers in this book who were able to participate in the two realities were also in the presence of a guide. Margaret Lewis Sauro's guide first walked along the flowered path with Margaret in her near-death experience and then accompanied her back to her hospital crib. Linda Allan was given solace by the Spirit People when she was in great pain in the hospital. Although this is not enough evidence to draw any conclusions, it would be hard not to indulge in a little speculation: such traversing of dimensions would be just what we would hope angels will help us do.

4. Her faith in that promise informed her decision forty-two years later when she had to decide whether or not to gamble on severe medical procedures for a life-threatening condition.

5. Luke 23:43.

6. The number 49 seems to have symbolic rather than literal significance.

Chapter 6

Where Is Heaven?

*Pure logical thinking cannot yield us any
knowledge of the empirical world; all knowledge
of reality starts from experience and ends in it.*

—EINSTEIN

*The physics of one period is the metaphysics of
the next.*

—MAX BORN

Blame it on Galileo. The whereabouts of
Heaven was easy before he grew curious about the sky. A thousand years before
him, Aristotle had divided the universe into
two realms: a decaying constantly changing
world below the moon and a perfect and unchanging world above. This theory suited
Christian theologians because they wanted
to place Heaven, as Scripture taught them
to, in Aristotle's serene astronomical sky.
This view of the universe is illustrated in
Martin Luther's Bible, published in 1534. In
the large center circle is a sweet view of
Adam and Eve standing in the Garden of
Eden with animals and fishes nearby. A thin

outer circle holds the sun and moon, puffy cumulus clouds, and a rim of stars. Outside this rim hovers God himself, looking like a friendly wizard gazing into his crystal ball. He is bathed in the radiant light of Heaven. The sky acts as a lovely unchanging cushion between earth and God's Heaven.

Seventeenth-century astronomers discovered that the actual sky refused to cooperate with this sweet view of the universe. Stars changed size, supernovas exploded, and comets no one had ever seen showed up. Such changes were a problem for theologians and astronomers alike. If the sky was constantly changing, it was not perfect. If the sky was not perfect, how could Heaven be there?

The biggest shock, according to Timothy Ferris in *Coming of Age in the Milky Way,* was the explosion of a supernova in 1604. The astronomical leaders of the day—Tycho Brahe, Kepler, and Galileo—were amazed that such a radical change could occur. Tycho Brahe, the first astronomer to spot the supernova, was so astonished that he decided his eyes must be at fault. But as the light from the supernova continued to glow for an entire year, astronomers had to acknowledge that it was not their eyes but the Aristotelian view of the heavens that was fading.

Myth has it that the bigger threat to Heaven had already occurred in 1543, when Copernicus published his view that the earth circled the sun—and not the other way around as the Bible contended. There is some truth to the myth: Copernicus himself was sufficiently worried that his discovery threatened the authority of the Bible, that he did not publish his ideas until he was on his deathbed. But Jacob Bronowski and others have pointed out that the Catholic Church did nothing to suppress Copernicus's book. It was not until Galileo trumpeted Copernicus's ideas and *turned a telescope on the night sky to prove them* that the theologians of the time felt threatened.

Although he is often given the credit, Galileo did not invent the telescope. He took—some say stole—the Dutch idea and realized its vast potential. Forty-five years old, sole provider for two sisters' dowries and sole support of a wayward musical brother, Galileo needed a boost to his income and his career. Luckily for both, he was mechanically minded and was able to devise how to enlarge and enhance the Dutch invention. He set up his handmade telescope in a balcony catercorner to the Doge Palace in Venice and invited all the Venetian senators to scan the seas for enemy ships. The senators understood immediately the strategic significance to their seafaring city. They doubled Galileo's salary and gave him tenure at Padua's university. His financial and academic security seemingly assured, Galileo trained his telescope on the night sky.

To Galileo's surprise, the telescope revealed, as the unassisted eye could not, that the sky had depth. Some stars were close, others were lifetimes away. If stars were at different distances, they were not studding the dome of Heaven as Aristotle had claimed. Galileo observed that we live in a gigantic universe—and Heaven was nowhere to be found.

At that moment, the history of Heaven's location became clouded. Rather than deal with the anxiety of Heaven's apparent disappearance, natural philosophers, as scientists were then called, sidestepped the issue. They argued that the Creator is too sophisticated for us to know him. They avoided talking about Heaven.

But near-death experiencers don't avoid the issue of location. They use the language of place freely. They speak of "going there" and "coming back." They speak of trees and grass and flowers. They describe the quality of the light and the fragrances that are new to them. Experiencers believe that what happened to them is *real*.

Anne Anderson, an elegant black woman who wears wide-brimmed hats and chic outfits in her time off, is the key triage nurse in a large medical practice. She manages both short-for-time physicians and needy patients with good humor and skill. It is hard to imagine her as an eleven-year-old fighting and screaming at emergency room doctors. She fought so hard that the medical staff finally put her under anesthesia in order to remove her thumbnail to extract a splinter.

As Anne recalls what happened next, "I went to this place that was really beautiful. There were all different flowers, yellows and greens and pinks, pansies and every kind of flower. Not very tall but really pretty. And the grass was green and the trees were green and beautiful, with a lake or pond with beautiful water. I wanted to stay there.

"I couldn't stay. There was a lady there, a tall lady. [Afterward] I kept telling my parents there was a lady there, because I used to tell them about it and they wouldn't believe it. They told me it was probably the anesthesia: 'You're just a kid. You couldn't be doing all that.' Because I told them about how I went through a tunnel and there was a bright light, and at the end of the tunnel there was this beautiful place with beautiful flowers and water. And it was such a beautiful place, I wanted to stay. But this lady told me I had to come back. So they [her parents] said, 'what lady?' So I described her. And they just couldn't believe it, because I wouldn't have known her. I said she was a tall lady with light skin and I said she had on a white top with a white long skirt. I told them exactly how she looked. I told them her facial features and that she was wearing a long white sash with a star on it. And they looked at each other and said, 'My God, she just described Big Ma.' Then they said, 'That was your great grandmother, and you wouldn't have known her.'

"I wouldn't have known her. And then they started to believe me. The star was the decoration of a Masonic lodge that she was buried wearing."

The moment of her parents finally believing the reality of her experience was, of course, hugely important to Anne. In the interview, she repeated the story several times, as experiencers often do, and then backed up a bit chronologically before proceeding. She went on, "I just said, 'Oh this place is so beautiful,' because I didn't notice anybody there. I was there alone. I was playing there. I was there by myself for a while. And I was so comfortable being there. I didn't want to go back. I wanted to stay where I was. But this lady said, 'no, you'll have to go back. I know you like it here, but you have to go back.' And I said, 'I don't want to go back.' And she said, 'but you have to.' She took my hand and was bringing me back. And then that was it."

Anne was brought up as a Southern Baptist. She had believed in the afterlife before her experience as an eleven-year-old and she believed in it afterward. The effect of the experience was to give her a sense of the place where she would be heading.

"I believe in Heaven and I believe in God," says Anne, now in her early fifties. "I'm not sure where I'm going, but I hope it is that place. If that's what it is all about, I'm ready to go now. That place was nice."

Is that "place" scientifically possible? For strict fundamentalists of any religion, God is capable of anything. Some might consider questioning the location of Heaven to be blasphemous. But for people of faith who are scientifically inclined, the problem of location is real.

Isaac Newton, the brilliant mathematician and astronomer, did not think that the scientific discoveries that he made put him in conflict with his faith. Born the year Galileo died, Newton was forced into seclusion on his mother's farm in 1665 at the age of twenty-three to avoid an epidemic plague that was sweeping

Britain. During that time he discovered his famous laws of motion and developed the theory of gravity. The planets' path that Galileo assumed was God-ordained was explained by Newton with gravity—another blow for God's image-makers.

This discovery was not a threat to Newton's own religious faith. Newton believed that the laws of gravity demonstrated that the universe was uniform and infinite. Because the Creator could hardly be less than the universe He created, Newton reasoned that God too must be infinite and everywhere.[1] This reasoning may be the most elegant and simple explanation of God ever argued. But there was still the problem of where to "put" Heaven now that Newton's theories confirmed without question Galileo's radical claim that Heaven was not in the sky. The only solution was to argue that we should not even ask about the location of Heaven. To want to know that Heaven is in a particular position is to place conditions on God.

The location of Heaven has been a dilemma ever since. That is not to say that people of faith or even theologians sat around puzzling about it. The location of Heaven was ignored. Deists like Benjamin Franklin and Thomas Jefferson were willing to give God the role of Watchmaker in the Sky, He who had wound up the universe. But they believed that we've been doing perfectly well without His intervention ever since. Our forefathers thought that if human beings could let go of their anxiety about sin and their obsession with an afterlife, the path of social progress would smooth out. They argued that if the universe was a well-oiled clock, quite unlikely to run down, then notions of the Apocalypse, Judgment, and Heaven were no longer relevant.

As Edward Harrison has pointed out in *Masks of the Universe*, when humankind began to care less about the rewards of Heaven, they cared more about the rewards of this earth. This shift has not been all bad. The nineteenth and twentieth centuries have seen a tremendous expansion of concern for the plight of people who are oppressed. Whereas the peasants of the Middle Ages or the slaves of the eighteenth century might have been willing to endure the hardships of serfdom, secure of their future in Heaven, farm and factory workers since then have insisted that they be compensated in this life for their labor.

The effect on the middle class may not have been as salubrious. If it is unclear that there is reward to come in the afterlife, the material rewards of this life become all-important. The size of one's paycheck, the accomplishments of one's children, the public recognition of one's efforts, and the length of one's obituary take the place of quiet good works observed by an all-seeing God who will mete out joyful compensation in Heaven.

Such reactions actually dovetail quite closely with ancient Egyptian views and modern Jewish views of immortality. "The king whose achievements are talked about does not die," claimed Sesostris I, a pharaoh of the second millennium B.C.E. The pyramids would stand as both accomplishment and memory for generations to come. Likewise, modern Jews are apt to believe that dead is dead. What will endure are one's accomplishments and the memories of love and deeds in those who live on.

When Heaven no longer has a place, Marx can argue that religion is an opiate and Freud can scoff that Heaven is mere wish fulfillment. When Heaven no longer has a place, even leading Christian theologians like Rudolf Bultmann, an influential German scholar, could propose that it is possible to be a Christian without believing in Heaven. Paul Tillich, possibly the most influential liberal Protestant theologian of our time, could sigh and say that all we can hope for is to dwell in God's memory.

But what about the near-death experiencers? Where do they *go?* Where is the other side of the tunnel? Does Heaven have a place?

It does. When Albert Einstein discovered relativity and Werner Heisenberg discovered the uncertainty principle, Heaven the place became possible again. An understanding of the differences between classical and modern scientists will help frame this discussion.

Classical scientists, who base their mind-set on Newton, believe that when they are studying something, they are studying what is out there, the actual thing that is. A classicist can measure a moon, discover a star, or inspect a virus and believe that is reality. As observers and participants in everyday life, we are all classicists by nature.

Classical scientists believe that everything is ultimately knowable. It is just a matter of time until the next layer of scientific understanding is uncovered. Classicists sometimes refer to God or Heaven, but as intellectual scaffolding, a shorthand for announcing the temporary limits of knowledge.

Quantum mechanics and modern astrophysics have challenged the belief that the world is knowable. Modernists, whose mind-set is rooted in the work of Einstein, claim that in fundamental ways certain knowledge of the world is inaccessible, even for the most sophisticated minds.

Consider the fourth dimension of space-time, the three dimensions of the senses that we know with time added. We look at the room that we are in and believe that we can measure the space. We look at our watches and believe that we can measure the time. Space and time appear as two distinct calibrations. According to relativity theory, they are not. As Einstein has said, "Time and space are modes by which we think and not conditions in which we live." Relativity theory integrated the two and showed that there exists a transcendent reality called four-dimensional space-time. As the science fiction mavens have been telling us, we should be able to move around in time in the same way that we move around in space.

Relativity is a radical departure from the classical, Newtonian, mind-set. It is terribly hard to accept that a fourth dimension exists that cannot be proven in the realm of the senses. Let's ratchet down one dimension to illustrate why it is so difficult to conceive of added dimensions.

Imagine you are a flat bug living a flat life on a flat white sheet of paper.[2] You are two dimensional. Imagine that a professor is trying to explain that there are actually three different dimensions in the world, and that if you—the flat bug—could just look on the other side of the sheet of paper you would see a sphere. But you can't see the other side of the paper; you are limited in your abilities to see anything more than two dimensions. The professor holds the sphere up to the light, so that at least you'll see the shadow of the sphere. Hah! you say. A sphere is the shape of a circle. The author brings the sphere right to the sheet until it touches. Hah! you say. The sphere is the shape of a dot. You would be accurate both times. A sphere does indeed have millions of dots on its surface, and it also describes millions of circles. But only if you could lift yourself out of your two-dimensional limitations of being a bug in Flatland could you metaphorically lift the sheet and see the whole, round sphere. In the same way, we who live in three dimensions find it nearly impossible to conceptualize added dimensions. There is a conceptual sheet of paper between us and four-dimensional space-time. We can understand space and we can understand time. It is terribly hard to imagine them together.

Imagine that the flat bug, who only lives in two dimensions, and a space bug, who lives in three, are having a race to see who can arrive at a point first. There is a long line between them and their destination that they are not allowed to touch. The flat bug will have to go around the long line to get to the point because he can only maneuver in two dimensions. The space bug, however, will be able to hop over the line. Not only will she probably win, she will seem to the flat bug to have utterly magical powers. Imagine the race from the flat bug's point of view: "The space bug was right here, and then she was gone. And then she reappeared on the other side of the line. Magic!"

It would not be magic, of course. It would simply be the flat bug's inability to perceive the reality of a higher dimension. In the same way, we who think we live in only three dimensions would think that anyone maneuvering in space-time was magic, mystical, or suspect.

This concept of moving about in higher dimensions does not seem to cause a conceptual problem for near-death experiencers as it does for us. When Warren Doe was negotiating with his angel-attorney during his life review, the angel would sometimes leave. As Warren explains it, "There was this blank spot when this person would disappear and I would just be there. And that's another thing that struck me. There was no time. It's not as if you're waiting for the person to return, because there is no time. It's like Gone. Back."

With all due respect to Warren, he sounds just like our hypothetical flat bug!

We have another limitation on our ability to understand the fullness of reality. Heisenberg has proven that we can measure the probability of a particle being in any particular place; we cannot pinpoint its whereabouts definitely. He also proved that the very act of looking at a particle changes the behavior of the particle. If the particle is acting like a particle, the act of looking at it will cause it to perform like a wave. A wave, once located, will behave like a particle. That's because particles and waves are not "really" mathematically different; it is the act of observation that makes them behave one way or the other.

Plato insisted that the reality of what we perceive is not in fact all of reality. Not surprisingly, Plato became unfashionable during the Newtonian era; classical Newtonian thinkers wanted to think that what we observe is what is true. Modernists, on the other hand, understand that the reality of what we perceive is not in fact all of reality but, as Plato contended, shadows on the wall of the cave.

That is bad news and good news for locating Heaven. The bad news is that we cannot ever locate Heaven with our senses, because we can never see the entire real world. We are only capable of seeing with our senses in three dimensions of the world. The good news for locating Heaven is that the reality of the senses within three dimensions is not the whole of reality. Heaven may very well be located in another "higher" dimension.

Welcome to the world of higher-dimension theory. Physicists themselves cannot "see" higher dimensions. What they can see is the effects of those higher dimensions. We cannot "see" a fourth dimension of space-time, but once Einstein proved it mathematically, physicists could explain why light curves. If a fifth dimension exists, it, too, has aspects that we cannot perceive, just as the flat bug could not perceive the sphere. Scientists do not yet "know" that the fifth dimension exists. But they do know that assuming one allows them to connect various forms of nature and unify those forces, which is what scientists are driven to do.

Einstein, for example, tried to unify the gravitational force with the electromagnetic force. He failed. But in 1919 a theory put forth by Theodor Kaluza and later by Swedish physicist Oskar Klein convinced Einstein that the two forces could be unified by postulating a fifth dimension.

What does the fifth dimension have to do with locating Heaven? The probability of a higher dimension allows for the possibility of still more aspects of reality. Heaven itself may, in purely mathematical terms, be above us, around us, in an infinite number of spaces in the fifth dimension.[3]

If the fifth dimension exists, early ideas about the location of Heaven that came to seem quaint within classical, Newtonian physics are now perfectly plausible. The Vikings called Heaven Valhalla and put it over the horizon. Tribes of Eskimos believed Heaven was under the sea where the fishing was always plentiful. Those who had suffered in this life rose into the Aurora Borealis where they could be seen in the shimmering lights. Who is to say they are not there? Discoveries in quantum mechanics and astrophysics make the Jewish concept of the "world beyond" and the Christian concept of "Heaven in our midst" utterly possible. Near-death experiencers shooting through tunnels, traveling at the speed of light, and arriving in other magnificent realms is also feasible. Even though we cannot prove the existence of Heaven, we can show that there is all the room in the world for its location.

NOTES

1. The notion that God is here, there, and everywhere was first argued in 1277 by the bishop of Paris, Etienne Tempier. His famous "condemnations" of contemporary religious thinking opened the door for Copernicus and would surely have been known to someone as educated as Newton.

2. I have borrowed this analogy from *Flatland*, an 1884 science fiction novel by English theologian Edwin A. Abbott. He is a favorite among astrophysicists.

3. String theory postulates ten or even as many as twenty-two dimensions. However, as this book goes to press, no one as yet has been able to make the math work. Whatever the fate of string theory, a fifth dimension, the math for which has been worked out, is sufficient for my argument.

✳ Chapter 7

Heaven and Health Care

THE KNAVE OF HEARTS: "I don't believe there's an atom of meaning in it."
THE KING: "If there's no meaning in it, that saves a world of trouble, you know, as we needn't try to find any. [But] I seem to see some meaning . . . after all."

—LEWIS CARROLL
ALICE IN WONDERLAND

Debbie was frightened. A twenty-six-year-old with a wonderful family and a husband she loved, she should have had her whole life in front of her. Instead she had terminal lung cancer. The disease had spread. Debbie was furious at her fate and terrified of dying. Over and over she said to the nurse who was working with her that she did not want to die and she did not understand why she had been chosen to die. Nothing the nurse or her family could do or say seemed to help. The nurse described Debbie as "petrified."

Six months after the initial diagnosis, Debbie developed a pulmonary embolism while at home that caused cardiac arrest. She had a blissful near-death experience. She arrived at the emergency room unconcerned about her physical state and totally elated. Her NDE had erased her fear of dying. She told her physician what had happened. He responded by telling her that she had had a psychotic reaction to the medications used during her resuscitation.

Debbie was outraged that the doctor was discounting an event that was utterly real to her. Luckily, the nurse that she had been working with, Diane Corcoran, was at the hospital at the time. She was called to the emergency room. Even luckier, Corcoran's own father had had a near-death experience and she was knowledgeable about the phenomenon. She told Debbie that her experience was a normal and natural aspect of dying. By honoring Debbie's experience, Corcoran restored Debbie's sense of joy at what she had learned during her near-death experience.

Debbie was transformed by the near-death experience and the affirmation she received from the nurse. She was no longer afraid of dying. She died in peace two days later.

Before she died, Debbie said something to her nurse that all health-care professionals need to hear. She said that it was deeply unfair that her health care or even the attitude toward her should be in any way compromised because of her NDE.[1]

With one exception, the experiencers interviewed who confided their near-death experience to a health-care professional were told that their experience was meaningless.

Imagine how this story might have unraveled if Debbie had not met nurse Corcoran, an army nurse and colonel stationed at Debbie's hospital at the time. What would have happened if she had been told without benefit of a sympathetic nurse—as most experiencers were—that her near-death experience was merely a hallucination, or oxygen deprivation, or a surge of endorphins to compensate for the stress on her heart? Like many experiencers, she might have decided to keep quiet about what happened and drawn on what she learned no matter what health-care professionals said. She might have reacted by doubting herself and the experience. At worst, she might have continued on the road of fear, denying her experience and her destiny, even demanding expensive, invasive, and ultimately fruitless medical intervention until the end.

One could say that it is time for the mystical path to be walked by those who wear practical shoes. Health-care professionals need to acknowledge the positive role of death-related visions. A near-death experience helped Debbie accept her impending death. It may have prevented costly and useless medical procedures from being ordered. These experiences should be affirmed whether or not health-care professionals believe that they are a forecast of the afterlife.[2]

Donna Pereira is a hospice nurse. She is a meticulously groomed woman with cautious eyes who was associated with the Visiting Nurses' Association. She prides herself on being practical. She understands her role as being there to tend to the physical needs of the patient, and maybe a few of the emotional needs. If anything more is needed, she calls in the social worker or the priest.

She had been working in a hospice for five years when she was assigned to Nora.[3] Nora had lived with her sister, Anne, all her life, even when they were both married. When Donna arrived at the house, the sister, Anne, needed help with several issues. She pleaded with Donna not to let Nora die. She also expressed exasperation that Nora was mentioning their older brother, Henry, constantly, insisting that she could see him. He had died several years before.

The hospice nurse explained that dying patients often see family members who have already died. Anne protested, saying that

Nora was talking and acting as if Henry were talking back. The hospice nurse asked if what Nora was saying would be appropriate to her relationship with her brother if he had indeed been present. The sister admitted that it was, but that she herself was being excluded from the conversation.

Although Donna did not believe in the afterlife, she knew from her hospice training to explain that what Nora was experiencing was natural and normal.[4] By honoring Nora's nearing-death awareness, she paved the way for Anne to find acceptance too.

On the third day that Donna came to help, Nora looked up at her and asked if she was dying. Donna told her the truth and asked her if she was afraid. Nora said she wasn't but that she had to make a decision. "I don't know if I should go to Henry or stay with Anne. I'm not scared. I just don't know what to do."

Anne stood by her sister, holding her hand.

A glazed look came over Nora's eyes, and the hospice nurse asked her what was happening. "Henry is touching me. Let go of my hand so I can touch Henry."

The hospice nurse had to encourage Anne to let go, and she asked Nora again what was happening. Nora said that Henry was touching her hand and telling her a hilarious story from their childhood. Nora was chuckling. Then the glazed look came over her face again, and Nora said, "I'm dying, aren't I? I'm going to have to leave Anne. Henry wants me."

In the three days since Anne had pleaded with the hospice nurse not to let her sister die, Anne had faced the inevitable. Anne hugged her sister and told her that she was free to go. Anne would miss her, but she would be fine.

Nora talked about the Light. In the distance she could see her mother, who had died years earlier. Nora did not talk to her mother, toward whom she felt more duty than love. She was focused on leaving with Henry. The hospice nurse was startled by

Nora's glowing smile and again asked Nora what was happening.

Nora talked about how warm and good she felt and said that she had no pain for the first time. She said that Henry was taking her down the road. "I need to go down the road. You need to let me go. I'm coming, Henry," said Nora. To her sister she kept saying, "Let go of my hand. I need to go."

Nora's sister was not holding on to her hand, so Donna wondered if the request to let go was symbolic. Other unresolved business might be keeping Nora alive. Donna called the family's priest and Nora's best friend. Nora ignored the priest but came out of her glazed look, eyes filled with joy, when she saw her friend. They hugged and talked of their many years of friendship. Nora thanked her friend for coming. Her eyes glazed over again. Suddenly she sat up in bed and told Henry that she was ready to go. Anne was letting her go. Then she died.

Donna Pereira's care for Nora and her family is a model of how health-care professionals might best respond to death-related visions. Her responses were respectful and sensitive both to Nora and her sister. As it turned out, her actions had benefits for Donna herself, too.

As Donna finished her account of her time with Nora, she slowed down, picking her words with care. She said, "Skeptics like myself say, sure. You die. You're put in a box and you're put in the ground, and that's the end of it. Whatever else happens is in your mind. But when you experience something like this, you have to face it. There is something. I don't know that it has anything to do with God or religion or our culture. But no matter whether it's religion or culture, I've got to admit there is something that gives people peace, and to want to go . . . it's nice to know there are two worlds. It's a comfort."

Donna had scorned belief in the afterlife all of her adult life. She questioned the teachings of her Catholic upbringing as a teenager and stopped attending church. Even the death of her son fourteen years before did not drive her to the solace of belief. She resumed attending church and taught Sunday School after her daughter was born, but she made a strong distinction between church doctrine and her own beliefs. She has tended to the needs of the dying and pronounced numerous patients dead, convinced that "You die, and that's it." But Henry's unseen presence changed her view. She now believes with conviction that there are two worlds.

In India, nearing death awareness is used to practical advantage. It is a Hindu tradition that when a family member dies at home, as most do, the room in which death comes must be closed off for three, six, and even sometimes nine months. Death is seen as a contaminant, which makes a great deal of common sense in a tropical culture. But it is also a Hindu value to include a dying person at the center of family life before his or her transition to the other side. The apparent conflict between these two values can sometimes be resolved by an understanding of nearing death awareness. Ramachandra Bhattar, a priest of a Hindu temple here in America, gave an example citing his own grandmother. When his grandmother could see deceased family members and angels hovering nearby, she let the family know that it was time to move her bed outdoors. The family stayed with the grandmother, attending to her needs, outdoors, until death came a few hours later. Honoring nearing death awareness prevented the necessity of an entire extended family—more than twenty people—moving out of the house after the death.

Patients' experiences of the transcendent deserve to be honored with the same respect by health-care professionals in Western cultures. Too often they are not. Little five-year-old Mary Olivia Pasterczyk was "pooh-poohed" by her doctors when she told them she had died during her bout with scarlet fever. Twenty-two-year-old Naomi Rosen had doctors who ascribed her near-death experience during cardiac arrest to her morphine drip.

Bettina Pratt fared slightly better with her physician. She was a teenager when she contracted encephalomyelitis. When she told the doctor that she had been "about to go into this beautiful place with the beautiful light," he believed her. But he also let her know that he thought she was a little strange.

Diane Komp is a pediatric oncologist and a professor at the Yale University School of Medicine in New Haven who, like Donna, "was somewhere between agnostic and atheist" when she finished her medical residency at Yale. She, too, has been deeply changed by what her patients have taught her. In the March 1992 issue of *Life* magazine (and in her subsequent book, *A Window to Heaven*) Komp tells the story of a seven-year-old girl dying of leukemia who sat up immediately before her death and said: "The angels, they are so beautiful, Mommy. Can you see them? Do you hear their singing, Mommy? I've never heard such beautiful singing." Then she died.

Komp learned from that child's death that whether or not we can prove near-death visions is irrelevant. The dying child's experience was enormously comforting to the mother and to the nurses on that ward who loved that little girl and were feeling the loss keenly. A child's death rips through our best attempts to weave meaning into death. A vision of angels helped the grieving process.

The little girl's vision helped her doctor, too. Komp has the grace to admit that it was a privilege for her to be present for it. She has since become a Christian. As Sherwin Nuland points out in his excellent book, *How We Die*, most primary-care physicians understand that they cannot wall themselves off from the spiritual issues of dying. They act as information source, sounding board, ethicist, minister. Yet there are too many stories in the death-and-dying literature that indicate that too many physicians are still uncomfortable with death.[5]

There are many reasons for their discomfort. Consider the

shadow side of a doctor's desire to be helpful. Medicine is a service profession. Physicians spend from early morning until late at night doing what they can to cure disease and alleviate suffering. By temperament they are doers. The central satisfaction of the job itself is being helpful. Physicians perform in high gear to solve problems.

But death cannot be solved. Death confronts all of us, and perhaps doctors most keenly, with our helplessness. When that helplessness is painful, doctors sometimes withdraw.

Sharing what near-death experiences teach us should become one last way for a physician to be helpful. Imagine the scene unfolding in two different ways. In the first, the doctor plays out one of medicine's most painful clichés. With the words "I'm terribly sorry—there is nothing more we can do," he purses his lips and turns away. He walks stalwartly down the long hall alone, while some family member of the about-to-die puts her head in her hands.

In the second scenario, family members are around the bed of the unconscious patient. The physician helps by explaining what is happening. Previously, she has encouraged the involvement of the family's minister, priest, or rabbi and is empathic and accepting of whatever religious beliefs the patient and family might share. She speaks gently and authoritatively. "Our evidence is that your grandfather is no longer in pain. When death comes, everything will smooth out. His face will relax. You may hear a rattle as he breathes his last breath. Don't be alarmed. It will not cause him pain. It is nature's way. Our information suggests that your grandfather may perceive himself moving into a warm and welcoming Light."

Family members nod. They feel comforted. Sensing this, the physician slips out, knowing that she has made a difference.

Near-death experiences are our largest and ever-growing

body of clinical knowledge about what it is like to die. We need to use that information for the solace it brings.

Parents of dying children who are knowledgeable about death-related visions do not allow health-care professionals to rob them of the comfort of near-death experiences. Jennifer Horacek was only sixteen when she died of cystic fibrosis, but she had taken a religion course the semester before in which she was assigned *Life after Life*. She had made a life review book for the course, fourteen pages of pictures and a little text. Her white cockapoo, Fang, figured most prominently on those pages. Her dog was her best friend.

Her family sneaked Fang into the hospital for Jenny on Christmas Eve. They wrapped the thirty-pound dog up in baby blankets and carried him up the back stairs. It was a happy evening for the Horacek family, with Jenny's brother and sister keeping watch at her door, hiding Fang under the bed when "unfriendlies" were spotted coming down the hall. When Fang died suddenly on January 17 of what turned out to be a massive tumor, Jennifer's mother, Sharon, decided they would not tell Jennifer.

Ten days later, after three months in the hospital and a bout with the respirator, Jenny did not want to endure it a second time. Her doctor talked her into it. Her parents wish they had not let the physician prevail. Says her father, Bruce, "Between the first and second stint on the respirator Jenny had talked to Sharon and used the words 'Gee, I hate to leave you guys, but I feel I just have to die.' We pretty much knew that it was all a matter of respecting her wishes . . . The doctor whom we had taken her to had a good longevity rate, and he found it very, very hard to give up. He always had more things to try. But then Jen had asked Sharon, 'Do you think I'll go into the Light?' So she was aware of that. That was nice. What it finally came down to was convincing the doctors that it was her wish not to try more extraordinary means. Basically, what Jenny wanted was to have us there, wanted to be held, touched, and wanted to be comfortable in terms of medication."

Jennifer was given morphine and Valium for her pain. She became unconscious between fifteen and thirty minutes later. Some things about the next three hours are very clear to her parents, some things are not. Says her father, "I remember suggesting that Sharon get in bed with Jenny, with Jenny leaning against her, and then I held her hands most of the time."

For some reason, he's not sure why, Bruce had brought Jennifer's life review book to the hospital. Nurses would come in and out those next few hours, and Sharon and Bruce shared the book with them. As Bruce remembers it, "There was a lot of reminiscing, and even laughing and tears, looking at the pictures of what was important to Jenny."

Something wonderful happened in those three hours. In the midst of the remembering, her mother cradling her, and her father holding her hands, Jenny lifted her hands and her father's into the air as though she were greeting someone. A physician came in and saw her hands lifting. He tried to ascribe it to dreaming or her CO_2 levels or oxygen deprivation. Bruce just looked at him and said, "I don't think so." Six times in those three hours, Jenny raised her hands. Her older brother said later she was reaching out to Fang.

"It was a very calm time, very peaceful," said her father quietly. "It almost seemed appropriate that she die then. After she died, we kind of looked back at that and asked ourselves, How did we let our child die and feel so peaceful?"

The physician in this case missed a chance to be helpful. At the very least, he could have asked why Jennifer's father did not think CO_2 levels were the cause of her hands' lifting. Instead of discounting the Horaceks' reality, the physician could have honored a moment of high spiritual significance for Jennifer's family.

Bruce is a professor of gerontology at the University of Omaha. Sharon is a therapist. After Jennifer's death they became involved in the International Association of Near-Death Studies, and Bruce currently serves on its board of directors. As he says, "That's why I got led into the near-death stuff. I had thought it (Jenny's death) was going to be such a mixture of feelings, and instead I felt like ninety to ninety-five percent something good was happening."

Like all parents of children who have died, Bruce and Sharon will never recover completely from the loss of their daughter. Bruce often refers to C. S. Lewis's powerful description in *A Grief Observed* of such a devastating tragedy as an amputation. You may adapt to the loss of a leg. The fierce and relentless pain may subside. But your life is forever changed. Every morning the leg is still gone. Every morning Jennifer is gone. But the image of Jennifer lifting her hands in greeting will sustain her parents all their lives.

Getting health-care professionals to acknowledge the spiritual in medical care may be a more achievable goal than it would at first seem. In July 1994, Associated Press ran an article saying that experts in the field of pain management in severely ill children find that a child's religious and spiritual background can be brought to bear in easing physical and emotional pain just as it can with adults. Health-care professionals working for the World Health Organization announced draft guidelines for easing pain in children with cancer. The guidelines recommend treating children with morphine and codeine when necessary, but they also recommend incorporating the child's spiritual background into care.

The article cites Dr. Diane Komp's experience involving a dying boy who engaged her in a conversation about prayer. He then very slowly recited his nightly prayer, concentrating on the words. "Now I lay me down to sleep. I pray the Lord my soul to keep. If I should die before I wake, I pray the Lord my soul to take." According to Dr. Komp, he lived the next day—his last—without pain.

The implied link between spiritual faith and pain management cannot be proven. Yet the fact remains that, for whatever reasons, this terminally ill child had a pain-free final day. The boy's beliefs may have been relevant to his medical care.

Spiritual convictions and death-related visions are powerful stuff. Unlike dreams or hallucinations, they tend to become stronger in their impact as time goes on. What harm to soul and healing process is done to those whose experiences are discounted?

Sharon Battle, a well-read, beautiful woman with natural henna-colored hair and sage green eyes, speaks in a gentle tone that belies a sharp and inquiring mind. A health-care professional, she is married to a Freudian psychoanalyst. Because her husband, and others in her profession, think that near-death experiences indicate psychosis, she believes that her career would be compromised if she were to admit publicly that she had a near-death experience. Her name has been changed.

Researchers in the field of near-death studies have determined that the aftereffects of psychosis and hallucination are dramatically different from the aftereffects of near-death experiences. Whereas those emerging from a psychotic episode are confused, anxious, and suffering from grave distortions in their perceptions of reality, near-death experiencers are lucid, alert, and often joyful.

Sharon's near-death experience was quite simple. She was twelve years old when she suffered a cerebral hemorrhage. She was hospitalized. Her parents and doctors thought she was going to die. Her own memory of the event is spotty. She just remembers seeing the Light. As she says, "My story is not so dramatic, but it was dramatic for me. The Light was very clear and it came for me, and it held the meaning of some kind of divinity. I didn't feel close to Jesus then, but it felt like God to me. It felt like it was saving me, and of course I didn't feel that I deserved to be saved. I was lying on a table in the room where they were going to do the surgery. It was scary. When the Light was there I knew that I was going to be all right, and I didn't need to be so traumatized. I was separate from the Light, but the Light made me part of it, even though it was on the other side of the room."

She also remembers being out of her body in the corner of the room. "I was in the corner of the room, and I was small. I was looking down at the room. And it didn't seem unusual at all. It seemed like the simplest thing."

Sharon says that she had no religious context within which to put her experience. Her parents were, by her description, "very materialistic," reacting against Southern Baptist Bible Belt mentality. Sharon does not mention ever telling them what happened. In the years since she witnessed the Light, Sharon has struggled with her memories. She tried discounting the memory, knowing that she was on medication at the time. She tried understanding it from a Freudian perspective and ascribed it to disassociation. Although it caused conflict for a time in her marriage, Sharon, with the help of counseling, has decided to affirm the experience. As she says, "I've had a lot of trouble trusting this whole thing."

Lehman Woods, on the other hand, displays not a shred of ambivalence about his near-death experience. The contrast between the two reactions may lie in differences in temperament. If Sharon is an orchid, then Lehman is an oak. But the difference in their reactions to their own respective NDEs is also a function of the reactions they received from health-care professionals. Whereas Sharon's experience was discounted, Lehman's was endorsed.

Lehman is an executive in a training and computer technology company. He feels "completely comfortable" telling anyone in his company, including his boss, about his experience. He is the only experiencer to feel no fear of being judged as odd. He is also the only experiencer of the fifty-one interviewed whose experience was affirmed by the health-care professional he told. This may be a coincidence. Maybe it is not.

For as comfortable as Lehman is in being public about having had a near-death experience, he took pains to mention the honors that his physician had accrued, emphasizing that he was one of the top in his field. Lehman also wanted to make it clear that he considers himself a rational man. He majored in business administration and had a double minor in religion and Russian studies in college. He has a master's degree in business administration. None of this kept him safe when he was a young man in a snowstorm.

Snow was coming down in drifts four days before Christmas 1975. Lehman was twenty-eight years old. He had been married for several years and had a good job as a cost engineer for General Dynamics' Electric Boat division. He was driving slowly on a country road in Rhode Island. The other car hit the driver's side door full force. Impact from the accident crushed Lehman's rib cage, punctured his left lung, and ruptured his aorta. Luckily, his aorta was not completely severed. He went in and out of consciousness as he arrived by ambulance at Rhode Island Hospital. In the pre-op room he left his body and went to the top left corner of the room.

In describing his experience, Lehman is precise about the location of the surgical table, the placement of various doors, and the relationship of his body on the table to various personnel entering and exiting the room. He believes that his specifying the layout provides proof that he witnessed the scene from a vantage point that was out of his body.

Lehman saw himself lying on a table in the center of the

room. The doors going into the operating room were on the right. The body—his body—was lying on its right side, facing the wall and away from the doors going into the operating room. The body was lying perpendicular to the doors going to other parts of the hospital. Lehman was later told that he was unconscious the entire time.

But Lehman did not experience himself as being unconscious. He recalls hovering at the top of the room having clearly conscious thoughts. "I remember spending time trying to figure out what was happening. There was no change in my mental state. I kept trying to reason out my disassociation with the body that was lying on the table. People were coming and going. I thought it was pretty interesting, but I didn't care whether the body survived or not."

At one point the anesthesiologist came in from the operating room and suggested that Lehman was probably around 5 foot 10, and weighed 195 pounds. His guess upset Lehman, who remembers "coming down into the body, saying 5 foot 8 inches, 160 pounds and then going back into the corner."

Linda Burnett, who also arrived at a hospital unconscious after a car accident, recounts a similar moment of reentering her body to give the surgeon information she felt he needed. It is not clear whether Lehman or Linda actually came out of unconsciousness or not. Linda's hospital records were checked for other reasons and no indication either way was found.

Lehman then remembers the chief resident coming in to look at the body. As Lehman says, "I remember thinking, if this is dying, I really feel sorry for the people who are living. I had such a sense of well-being and comfort with myself."

Since his experience, Lehman has been exposed to the near-death literature and contrasts his with what he has read. "I did not have a tunnel experience or a companion or a bright light. It just seemed to me that an awful lot was going on and I was really having a good time. It seems to me that I remember a time of floating and a sense of light and smoke."[6]

Lehman recalls making a decision as they were wheeling him into the operating room. "I remember thinking, 'Oops, I better give this guy a chance,' and going back into the body."

Lehman does not recall anything more after he chose to go back into the body. His doctor, who was both chief of surgery and chief of cardiovascular surgery, told him later that they lost him several times in the operating room.

A key aspect of Lehman's experience for him was the visit his surgeon paid him several days after the operation. It was Christmas Eve. Lehman chided his doctor good-naturedly, saying that the surgeon should be home with his family instead of roaming the halls of the hospital. In a response that Lehman still recalls with great emotion, the surgeon told him that most of his trauma patients don't make it, and that Lehman himself should not have made it. He had come in to visit because it was successes like Lehman that made his job worthwhile.

So Lehman told the surgeon about his experience. The surgeon asked him to describe the anesthesiologists. Lehman characterized one as an Indian, about five feet seven, who came into the room from the operating room. He described the other as a taller man of Indian descent who was much less patient and tolerant with the nurses.

The surgeon confirmed Lehman's descriptions. He said that there was no possible way for Lehman to have seen the two men he described. Besides the fact that he was unconscious for the duration of his time in surgery, his body was facing the wall, away from those attending to him.

Lehman is not sure he would put a religious spin on his experience. He says, "To me this experience has nothing to do with faith. I know that what we are is not how we are manifested now, as surely as I am talking to you on the phone. Now every day, every single day that we have in this body is a gift. But that is not what, or who, we are. I'm not exactly sure what or who we are, but I know it is not what is walking around on earth. *The experience was too clear and ratified in so many different ways.* It was real. The fact that we cannot explain it yet is of no consequence to me."

The significant sentence in this last quote is the one in italics: "The experience was too clear and ratified in so many different ways." The surgeon's confirmation of Lehman's experience was terribly important to him. Whether or not the surgeon "believes" in near-death experiences in general is irrelevant; his affirmation of Lehman's had a demonstrably positive effect on Lehman. This respect for the patient's reality needs to spread among health-care professionals.

There is plenty of evidence that near-death experiences promote psychological and spiritual healing. Perhaps the most dramatic examples come from the renewed desire to live on the part of experiencers who have tried to commit suicide.

Bruce Greyson, Head of Psychiatry at the University of Connecticut Health Center and the editor of the *Journal of Near-Death Studies* did pioneer work in the early 1980s studying the effects of near-death experiences on suicide patients. One might expect that suicide patients who have blissful death-related visions might be even more disposed to try to take their lives again. Greyson found statistical evidence that near-death experiences have the effect of discouraging future suicide attempts. Among the reasons given by experiencers are a sense of having merged with the whole, "decathexis" from problems, and belief that life is precious and meaningful.[7]

The reactions of the experiencers interviewed who attempted suicide reinforce this finding. Steve Miner tried to drown himself, during which attempt he had a profound near-death experience. Although intellectually he still believes that everyone has the basic right to end his or her own life, he cannot imagine doing so himself. He says, "I tend to see life as a spiritual learning experience. My views on death and dying and what that's all about, which in my estimation is one of the most profound things you can glimpse any understanding of, have changed my outlook tremendously. So although it [suicide] is an option, it is not an option unless in some incomprehensible way I would be forced into it."

Warren Doe is another experiencer who has put himself to the test and come up with the same response. A decade after his failed suicide attempt, his life fell apart a second time. His wife had died, and he was about to begin a two-year prison sentence. Warren knew that prisons have their own kind of pecking order. According to him, if you murder someone you have quick seniority. His particular crime would be considered "the lowest of the low," and he would be treated accordingly by other prisoners. He was deeply frightened of going to prison. He put a .30-.30 revolver in his mouth for an hour with his finger on the trigger.

Says Warren now, "What stopped me was my near-death experience. I was reviewing it. I know the value of life. There is nothing that can happen on earth that can justify that action. I put the gun down and that was it."

The angel-attorney in his near-death experience had told him he had something important to do on earth. Warren believes it may have been nursing his wife, or maybe his art. It may simply be being the son who helped his parents with their transition into a nursing home even though his father condemns him for his past. Says Warren, "The point [of the near-death experience] was you have not done what you're supposed to do yet. Shape up and get with it."

A decision to forgo the option of suicide is the most dramatic form of psychological healing. Near-death experiences can promote other kinds of healing as well. Bill Pacht is manager of engineering and computer services at a large aerospace company. He is in charge of all personal computers, computer networks, and engineering computer services in the corporation. It is an extremely high-stress job. Bill has the "Type-A" personality to handle it. He and his wife are childless; they had an active nightlife. Bill enjoyed the "good life." He sported a Rolex watch, took his vacations from New England in Miami, and was saving for a Corvette when he had his near-death experience at the age of forty-one.

Bill thought he was in great physical shape in the spring of 1993. Two years before, he had bicycled the length of Florida down to Miami. He called his bicycle trip his "great midlife adventure." He had good reason to seize the time. His grandfather had died at the age of forty-seven. His father also had died of a heart attack at the age of forty-seven before Bill's eyes when he was twenty.

His father's death has taken a toll on Bill. "That was brutal, because we were at war," he says now. "Total war. I never called him Dad. When he died, that was hard for me."

The effects of the loss go on and on, by his own poignant admission. As he says, "For the last twenty years I've been dwelling on dying."

For the past five years Bill had a feeling something was going to happen to him. As he says, "I was calling up people I hadn't seen in twenty years and saying hello and good-bye. I mean I was cleaning out my closets, throwing away my *Playboys*."

One day in July 1993, he heard what he calls his inner voice, vehement and insistent, and he didn't like what it said. "I was sitting watching TV when this strong, strong voice comes over me and says, 'It is time to go' [to the hospital]. And I said, 'I'm not going.' Like I was arguing. And it says, 'you're going.' So I went. And then everything happened."

One of Bill's coronary arteries was 98 percent blocked. He

was transferred to a larger hospital that specializes in cardiac problems, where he submitted to two balloon angioplasty procedures. The procedures failed. Two days later, he underwent bypass surgery.

The last thing Bill remembers is going under the anesthesia. Then he found himself sitting about ten feet away from the operating table on what seemed to be a filing cabinet, watching the whole operation. As he describes it, "Emotionally, it was weird. I remember thinking, 'Well, this is pretty cool.' I wasn't excited, I wasn't depressed. Just really matter of fact. Well, this can't be a dream."

He had always known, because of his family history, that he was probably going to have to have surgery at some point. He had always imagined what would happen. This wasn't it. He tells what occurred: "So I'm sitting there watching the whole thing when my mother, who is dead, and my uncle, who is dead, come into the room. My mother was a chief operating nurse back in the late forties in New York, and her uncle was chief surgeon in a hospital out in Chicago. And they come into the room, right? And they go into the bodies of the people who are working on me.

"It was weird. We communicated. But not verbally. I don't know if I want to say telepathically. She knew everything I was thinking right away, and I knew everything she was thinking. One of the things I said was 'What are you doing here?'

"She said, 'We're here to fix you up.'"

Bill was fascinated by his uncle's and mother's hands. They were moving really fast, helping the surgeons perform the operation. Bill did not feel particularly surprised to see his mother. He had often sensed her spirit around the house. He asked her where she had been.

She said, "I live in Chicago now."

Bill said, "Why are you living there?"

His mother replied, "You don't get to choose where you go. You're assigned."

Her answer surprised him. "I thought that was weird. I've never really had that thought process before. This went on for a while. Next thing I remember, I was in the recovery room, watching this. I don't remember it as a participant. I remember standing there watching it. I'm lying there, looking up at the nurse, who's got me, who's waiting for me to come up out of the anesthesia. I'm looking at her and she's strobing. She's got short blond hair and my mother had gray fake hair and I'm looking at her and she's strobing between her and my mother, her and my mother, real fast. I'm yelling at her about Chicago. Later they asked me, 'Why did you keep yelling about Chicago?' That's when I said 'I remember all that.'"

During his experience, Bill believes that his mother and uncle took him to another place entirely: "They were kind of finishing me up. And they took me to this room, and I was all of a sudden in this place. And the room was funny, like a big conference room. It wasn't flat. The floor was slanted. In this room was a big table, oval. There were a lot of people in there. Some of them I recognized. Some of them I didn't. But they were supposedly all family members. And there was this chair in one of the corners up at the top. Something about that was going to be my spot. I don't know what that means."

Bill felt odd about his next admission: he had the feeling that he was taught that family members can give up parts of their lives to contribute them to others. He was given the impression when he went to the room that they were waiting for him and that he was "the leader of the tribe." He felt that all those people had taken up a collection of aspects of themselves, giving things like time so that he could be in this life longer.

"My mother's hands were moving real fast. She was doing

things these guys don't even know about. They were doing their thing. I had the best surgeon around. But she knew stuff he didn't know. She's doing stuff, and undoing stuff they're doing and I felt really good about it, like I know I'm going to live as long as I want to.

"Part of this was she put me at peace. She said, 'You don't have to worry about this stuff anymore. You're going to take care of yourself and you're going to live to be a certain age . . . seventy-two.' Which is unusual for men in my family."

Bill was given a forecast of his mortality that is longer by three decades than his father's. This forecast may have significant consequences in terms of Bill's health, whether or not it is "true" that he will live to seventy-two.

Topnotch research has been done to show that a doctor can use his or her power to expedite the healing time of a patient. In an article published in the *British Medical Journal*, K. B. Thomas provides persuasive evidence that if a doctor suggests that a patient will get well, and quickly, the patients to whom that suggestion has been made improve dramatically faster than patients who have not been given such optimistic forecasts.[8]

Dr. Michael Sabom is a cardiologist and staff physician at the Atlanta Veterans' Administration Medical Center, and, as the author of *Recollections of Death,* is one of the most renowned researchers in near-death studies. He is currently developing a research model to evaluate the effects of a divine authority telling a patient during a near-death experience that it is not his or her time to die. His hypothesis is that such experiencers, like the fast-healing patients whose doctors told them they would get well quickly, will also reveal faster rates of healing than a control group of cardiac-arrest patients who had not had near-death experiences. If his research proves his hypothesis, Sabom will have gone far in proving that transcendent near-death experiences play a natural and beneficial role in the healing process.

Bill Pacht fits this model. Convinced because of his mother's message during his NDE that he is to live much longer than he had ever thought possible, Bill is doing everything he can to make her prediction come true. He has changed his diet, lowered his stress, and adapted his lifestyle toward achieving that aim. If Sabom's hypothesis is correct, Pacht's near-death message, coupled with his optimism and proactive attitude, would actually speed up the healing process.

In a stress test taken a year after the surgery, Pacht passed Level 5, the top level of exertion on a stress test. His doctor told Pacht that only 3 percent of all bypass surgery patients ever pass Level 5. Until otherwise proven, it would seem foolish in the extreme to undercut such an encouraging blessing about future health conveyed during a near-death experience.

In health-care terms, the best of the death-related visions are interactive. The patients share the stories with the health-care professional, who honors the story to help the patient—and sometimes benefits the health-care provider as well. For too long, near-death experiences have been the odd or treasured secret of experiencers. The skepticism that caused that secrecy should end. Both in grieving and in the healing process, near-death experiences are helpful in medically practical ways.

NOTES

1. Debbie's name has been changed. I heard her story from Diane Corcoran. See the next note.

2. This chapter would not have been written if I had not attended the 1994 annual conference of the International Association of Near-Death Studies. I am indebted to Diane Corcoran, R.N., Ph.D.; Melvin Morse, M.D.; and Michael Sabom, M.D. for their lectures on the medical issues of death-related visions. For more on this subject, read Melvin Morse's article in *Current Problems in Pediatrics* 24, no. 2: 45–92 (February 1994).

For a nursing perspective, listen to Diane Corcoran's tape, "NDE— Perspectives and Strategies for Health-Care Professionals." It is available through IANDS, P.O. Box 502, East Windsor Hill, CT 06028. Sabom's book on the subject is forthcoming.

3. Donna's own name has not been changed, but Nora's name and those of her relatives have been changed, at Donna's request, to protect their privacy.

4. Besides the training Donna had as a hospice nurse, she also had the advantage of reading Maggie Callanan's seminal book, *Final Gifts*. Callanan coined the expression and provided persuasive examples of nearing death awareness.

5. To explore this subject further, read *On Death and Dying*, by Elisabeth Kübler-Ross, or just about anything of the hospice literature. Also good is *The Silent World of Doctors and Patients*, by Jay Katz.

6. Researchers have to worry about the possibility of experiencers embellishing or dovetailing their experiences to the literature after reading about NDEs. Lehman's narrative rings true, in part because of his use of the word *smoke*. Such a description is unusual.

7. Greyson first presented these findings at the 1982 annual conference of IANDS in Charlottesville, Va. His findings were published in "Near-Death Experiences and Attempted Suicide," *Suicide and Life-Threatening Behavior* 11 (1981):10–16.

8. K. B. Thomas, "General Practice Consultation: Is There Any Point in Being Positive?" *British Medical Journal* 294 (1987):1200–1201.

Chapter 8

What Happens When People Who Don't Believe in Heaven Have NDEs?

Life is pleasant and I have enjoyed it, and I have no yearning to clutter up the Universe after it is over.

—H. L. MENCKEN

All my life I haven't believed in the afterlife, and I don't like to be wrong.

—ELINOR FINKELSTEIN, EXPERIENCER

Linda Burnett was an atheist, "the kind that would argue with you," as she put it, about God. She had completely rejected her Catholic upbringing. She believed that death is like a leaf falling from a tree. The leaf decomposes on the ground and becomes part of the earth again. That's it. But her beliefs could not explain what happened to her on April 25, 1975.

She had just gotten off the graveyard shift in a coal mine in Colorado. In the process of divorcing her husband and suddenly singly responsible for providing for two small children, Linda had found coal mining to be the only decent-paying job she could get. She was driving over Berthoud Pass in the Rocky Mountains of Colorado to go to the laundromat and then look for a new apartment, when she should have been at home in bed. She fell asleep at the wheel on a mountain switchback and drove right off the pass. Linda woke up as the back wheels left the road. The car was falling into the ravine below.

Out loud, sailing through the air, Linda said, "You dumb bitch—you just killed yourself." Her next reaction was to recall her Catholic upbringing. She remembered being taught in Sunday School that "if you called on Jesus when you were dying, you would go to Heaven." She said to herself, "There's no time like the present to check this out." So she yelled, "Oh, Jesus," laid her head in the passenger seat of the car, and waited to die.

"The next thing I knew I was zooming at incredible speed through what seemed at the time like a Quonset hut. But I'm an army brat, so someone else might look at it as a tunnel. It had lumpy, ripply walls with a tiny, tiny light at the end of this thing. I can remember thinking that the pinpoint should be getting bigger because I'm going so fast. It never got any bigger, but I popped through it."

From that moment, Linda's perspective changed completely. "At that point I was above the trees, in the same place at Berthoud Pass, but I was looking at the sky and the trees and the mountains. It was the most incredibly beautiful sight I've ever seen, because I could see not only in front of me and peripherally, but I could see behind me, above me, and below me. Completely spherically. I could see miles and miles. I was so taken by the beauty of Colorado."

Linda was not registering that anything except the beauty was unusual about her perspective. But then she looked below her. "As I looked down, enjoying my view, I saw all these people standing at the edge of the road looking down. My thought was, I wonder why they are looking down when everything to really see is up here. Everything is so beautiful. So I decided to look at what they were looking at. That's when I saw a car, upside down with the wheels still spinning. And I could see this body hanging out of the car. And I thought, is that what they're looking at? And then I thought, oh, I was driving a car like that, and then I thought well that's me hanging out of the car. But if that's me, oh my gosh I'm dead."

Linda's perspective then changed a second time. As she describes it, "Instead of feeling bad about it, or wondering about it, it was kind of a joyful experience. I was euphoric. It was almost as if I were swimming underwater and I surged. The next thing I know I'm in a whole different place and this place is also filled with light, but it also had a cacophony of business going on. It's got movement, and it's got light, and it's got sound, and it is very, very active and busy. I felt as if I were spinning in this place. The only way I can describe it is like building a La-Z-Boy recliner with an erector set and I'm in it. I was in a relaxed position cruising around enjoying myself. I don't remember being focused in any one place or being spoken to or thinking. I just felt the contact of it."

All of a sudden Linda again "bolted," this time out of the spinning-in-the-noisy-light perspective back to "floating and bobbing" in the sky. She was back in the Berthoud Pass area. However, she was no longer interested in the scene on earth. As she remembers it, "Instead I'm looking at a very long line of single-file spherical lights. I will call them bubbles for lack of a better term. You might call them the energy of a soul. I don't really know what they were."

Twenty years later, Linda still does not know what to think of the tiny lights. Another experiencer, Diana Wood, encountered the same tiny twinkling lights and felt certain that they were souls.

Whatever they were, Linda was impressed. "It was single file and there must have been a zillion of them in the sky, lined up like a wedding reception line."

According to Linda, the lights seemed headed into the glacier that is on the Pass. She decided to join the line. "It was as if I was coming up to the light at the end of the line to be introduced. That was the feeling I was getting: Oh, I'm going to meet these people, although of course there weren't any people."

Just then Linda was told by a voice that a certain person needed her. The exact words were "He couldn't make it without you." It was a person she knew well, a good friend whom she later ended up marrying and eventually divorcing. Linda laughs about it now: "At the time I didn't understand it, and I'm not sure I do now."

She was sent back into her body immediately after hearing the voice.

The voice that Linda heard was the most difficult part of the experience for her to make sense of and accept. During the year after the accident, Linda decided that it had been her friend's deceased mother who had spoken to her. But now she is not so sure. She worries that she may have come up with that explanation because "it was easier to believe that a ghost might have spoken to me than to believe that God, or Goddess, or some other Spirit reality might have been with me."

The fact of the voice forced Linda to reexamine whether she believed in God. As she says, "I had a real confused perception of what was going on, but I didn't doubt that it had happened."

Linda's experience unraveled her atheism. In the aftermath of her near-death experience, she could no longer justify her rejection of God or the afterlife.

Linda has gone from being an atheist to being a New Age spiritual seeker. She now has an active religious life. She reads stones and believes in shamans and the power of meditation. She has even regained a measure of respect for the Catholic Church, although its politics "annoy" her. Linda is now involved in the Church of Religious Science, a nonsectarian church in her area.

Linda's experience dismantled the power of death for her. She now believes that nothing ends: "We retain our sight, our hearing, and most especially our thought." As she says, simply and firmly, "We do not die."

Interviewing an atheist who came to believe in God and the afterlife as a result of a near-death experience invited new perspectives. It's one thing for an experience to confirm a person's most deeply held religious reliefs. Only a few of the experiencers fit that description. Most of the experiencers grew up in a tradition of belief but had become agnostic. They did not know what they thought and they did not care. Now they know. The pendulum had to swing even farther for Linda, who let go of her atheism for a world view that could embrace her experience rather than dismiss it.

But even with Linda, it could be argued that in time of crisis or danger, the most zealous iconoclast will regress to childhood beliefs. As the saying goes, "there are no atheists in foxholes." While Linda's practicality in calling on Jesus as she sailed off the cliff was admirable, the question still remained what the effect of a near-death experience would be on someone who had *never* believed in Heaven.

Most Jews in contemporary times are not taught to believe in the afterlife. Most Jewish people will say that when you die, it's over. What lives on is the memories others have of the good work you have done in this life and the love you have created. It is completely possible to be an observant Jew—someone who lights the candles of Shabbat, keeps the Sabbath and the high holidays, and holds to a kosher diet—without believing in the afterlife. One of the most historically minded religions, Judaism may draw as much holiness from its rituals as from beliefs. For a Jew living in contemporary times, Jewish culture can be as important as faith. For some, culture is more important.

So what happens when a modern Jew who has been raised to believe there is no Heaven has a near-death experience? Only one Jew had volunteered to be interviewed. Several people familiar with the database of the International Association of Near-Death Studies admitted that of thousands of experiencers, they knew only two! If the only people who had near-death experiences were those who were brought up to believe in the afterlife, the seemingly impressive statistics about post-NDE belief in the afterlife would no longer be persuasive. But one of the two cited was Barbara Harris, a high-profile Jewish experiencer who has written a book, *Full Circle*, about the impact her near-death experience has had on her life; there had to be others. By word of mouth, six Jewish experiencers were found.[1]

Elinor Finkelstein was brought up in a Conservative Jewish household. She attended religious services and was confirmed. She describes her parents as cultural Jews who were big supporters of the synagogue, but she feels quite certain that her father did not believe in God. He was an Ethical Culturist. Elinor's husband has never really participated in organized religion with her. But they, too, kept Shabbat and celebrated the Jewish holidays. Both daughters were bat mitzvahed, and, as Elinor says, "We make a big thing of Passover, which my husband says he doesn't like, but I'm sure he does."

Elinor is a thoroughly modern Jew in her beliefs. "Dead is dead," she says. "I had always thought, and still do, that your immortality consisted of how you led your life on earth and how you are remembered. Therefore you should try to do the best you can while you are here."

By any standard Elinor was leading the good life at the time of her experience. She and her husband own a travel agency together which lets them indulge in their passion for traveling. Late October of 1976 found them in northern Spain driving on a narrow road with no shoulder to the Alhambra, one of the country's great historic sites. It began to rain very slightly. A driver coming from the opposite direction lost control of his car and crashed head-on into their tiny Fiat.

Elinor suffered internal injuries from the thrust of her body on impact against the seat belt. She was in great pain. A newspaper editor from the coast who stopped at the scene of the accident rushed them to Grenada, the nearest city. At the hospital, they determined that she was bleeding internally and needed exploratory surgery. It turned out that her liver had been lacerated and the bile duct was almost severed. After sixteen days in the hospital she was practicing walking in the hall when she became extremely dizzy from an arterial hemorrhage in the liver.

As Elinor remembers what happened, "Suddenly I had this very strange experience, feeling that I had left my body. I was able to see everything that was happening in the room, including seeing myself in bed. I wanted to tell my husband not to worry, and to comfort him, but I didn't have any speech. He looked like if I touched him he was going to shatter. Finally they were running me down the hall and I was looking up at these terribly dirty dingy ceilings. I remember telling my husband not to worry because Jewish women don't die in a place like this."

Elinor describes what happened as "a seesaw kind of thing. First I would drift, and then when I came to some kind of consciousness, I realized my circumstances. Then I was disappointed to be dying, but I was aware that I was dying."

During one of the out-of-body phases, Elinor went through to what she describes as "an area with some degree of light. But it wasn't what people tell you, and I didn't hear any music or any-thing like that. But it was like a light corridor. And when I got to the end, our father was there. Of course my father had died in the early sixties, and he was a very gregarious guy. All he said to me was, 'Sweetheart, don't come.'"

Elinor's sister had flown over from France to be with her while she was in the hospital. The next day, when Elinor told her about seeing her father, they both found it "the eeriest thing imaginable. It was so out of character for him," says Elinor, laughing. "We couldn't imagine that he wouldn't have wanted company!"

Seeming contradictions in near-death experiences—those mo-ments when something happens that goes counter to the experi-encer's expectations—are one of the more intriguing aspects of the phenomenon. George Jehn, who had only known his best friend Tom as bald with the diabetes that killed him, gets choked up every time he describes seeing his deceased friend during his near-death experience with a full head of curly dark hair. Elinor's father loved having friends and family around. The fact that it still seems odd to Elinor that her father would have turned down her company gives credence to the possibility that her vision is not simply a construct of her imagination.

When Elinor came to in the recovery room after the second operation, she was alone and scared. The seesawing in and out of awareness had left her disoriented—she did not know whether she was alive or not. She started to feel her body with the one hand that was free and realized that she was still wearing her own night-gown and robe. She thought to herself, "My God, you're dead. You must be dead. No one ever had surgery wearing her own clothes."

She was terribly upset because the nightgown that she was wearing did not match her robe. "I thought, 'I'm going to have to wander through all eternity wearing a dirty outfit that didn't match!' And the other thing was that I was furious because I had never believed in an afterlife, and I don't like to be wrong."

Elinor then felt her new set of bandages and realized she was alive. In their haste to operate, the doctors had just slit open her clothes.

Although Elinor felt confused in the transitions in and out of other dimensions, she was left feeling very clear about dying itself. "I want to stress that when all of this was happening, I did not find that it was very frightening to die," says Elinor now. "I thought that it was actually quite pleasant. Half of my head found the drifting toward death a very peaceful kind of a feeling. Every once in a while as I drifted back into life, I really didn't want to die because my youngest daughter was nowhere yet. I figured that my husband would grieve terribly, but he was still a young and handsome man, and he would pick up his life. And my older daughter was in medical school and she was married and I felt that she was okay. It was just this youngest daughter. And if she didn't need me, I needed to see how she was going to turn out. She had just started college, and I considered her unformed. I wanted to see what she would be.

"At times (during the seesawing) I did not want to die. I was very young. I was only forty-six years old. The other part of me, when I drifted, found it very very pleasant. And I will tell you, based on that experience, I would never ever fear death again. I do tell other people it's nothing to be afraid of. It's kind of nice."

Elinor found her near-death experience very unsettling. For six months afterward she dwelled on issues concerning life and death and felt impatient with issues of less weight. With her husband's help, she shook that attitude. Says Elinor, "My husband is very wise, with two feet planted firmly on the ground. And he told me, you know, people just don't live up there with these big values."

One day she was trying to deal with a client's complaint about the lack of a closet in the stateroom on an ocean liner. As she says, "I heard this harping, complaining, nagging, narrow-minded person—and it was me! And I knew I was better."

Elinor may indeed have been "better," as in back to her old self on a day-to-day basis, but her near-death experience has created lasting conflicts for her in her beliefs about the afterlife. She herself admits that she contradicts herself.

"It was really a very unsettling thing to be so close to death and to have this near-death experience when you had pooh-poohed all this. So I read this book [*Life after Life*]. And I don't pooh-pooh things as much as I did in the past. I'm not still 100 percent clear or sold about a lot of things I have read that other people have experienced. Things have happened to me. I mean, I think I'm still fighting the idea of a spirit world. I think that there are a lot of things that happen for which we don't have explanations."

Elinor was asked if she still thought death is final. "I'm not sure," she answered. "I'm really not sure having had this experience. The main thing is, it doesn't frighten me. Because my father didn't look unhappy to me."

Many of the twentieth century's most significant psychological thinkers, including Sigmund Freud and Otto Rank, believed that we construct different notions of the afterlife to combat our fear of death. These thinkers believed that fear haunts every one of us from the moment we are conscious. In *The Denial of Death*, Ernest Becker argues that fear of death is the driving force of a person's life. Clearly, these thinkers never met Elinor.

Elinor had *liked* the idea that she was going to be allowed to rest at the end of her life. She finds it disconcerting that her spirit may continue on. As she said, "I think for a lot of people who have lived a very long time and had a hard life, or whatever, it was so peaceful drifting toward this death, that it may be a very nice thing to rest, you know, to have it all over with. I haven't noticed that life has been extremely easy . . ."

Elinor was asked if her near-death experience means that she had to wonder whether or not there may in fact be an afterlife. She answered, "Absolutely. I think I have spent an adult lifetime simply being unwilling to allow these ideas in."

Elinor explained that eight years after her near-death experience her life was changed by grief. Her firstborn, her married daughter, a high-achieving physician, graduated from her medical residency and killed herself. As far as Elinor was concerned, the tragedy was a "nail in God's coffin." But given her experience seeing her father, she has had to wrestle with whether or not she will see her daughter again. As Elinor says, "I'm just saying that even when she died, I never really believed that I'm going to see her again. I think it would be nice. Other times I think I would yell at her. To see him [her father in the NDE] just shattered all my firm opinions about the afterlife. I told you, I really don't like being wrong. But it was just such a crazy thing for Daddy to say. But I saw him so clearly. That was the thing that was very unsettling. I also got a little frightened then because I was really very close to death or I wouldn't have seen him."

Elinor continues to live with the uneasy contradictions between her heritage and her experience. On the one hand, she would like to be able to stand by the firm convictions of a lifetime of death's finality and be able to count on the endless dreamless sleep that such a belief implies. On the other hand, the vision of her father was so clear and so real that she has to admit the possibility that there are other dimensions of reality. Rather than dismissing one or the other, she honors both. It has been said that ambivalence is the most truly adult emotion: that where children tend to see issues and choices as black and white, adults understand the painful grayness of life. Perhaps Mahatma Gandhi put it best when he said, "I have never made a fetish of consistency. I move from truth to truth."

For a religious tradition that has always relished paradox, Judaism, of all the great world religions, has certainly moved from truth to truth. The Pentateuch, the first five books of the Bible that are a sacred text (the Torah) for Jews, contains numerous references to Heaven. One of the most dramatic occurs in Genesis, involving Jacob. What a night that must have been for a future patriarch! Out in the desert, a rather callow young man on his way to the big city to seek a wife, Jacob resigns himself to a hard night's sleep with only a rock for a pillow. As is so often the case, spiritual revelation came in the midst of his isolation and loneliness. Jacob has his great dream of angels sliding up and down the ladder and his vision of Heaven. He said, "How awesome is this place. This is none other than the house of God, and this is the gate of Heaven!"[2]

Yet most Jews in contemporary times, like Elinor, have not been taught to believe that Heaven exists. The *Encyclopedia of Judaica* does not even have a listing for Heaven. The reason is more political than spiritual. In the 1600s, a false messiah drew tremendous and harmful power from his knowledge of the Kabbalah, mystical texts that described the Jewish belief in Heaven. The elders of the faith decided that to prevent such destructive power from erupting again, access to the Kabbalah would be limited. Only those who were forty years old, married, and thoroughly knowledgeable in the Torah would be allowed to study it.

That decision excluded all but a small elite. Women, for example, did not have access to the Kabbalah because they were not allowed to study the prerequisite Torah. As prime bearers of culture, they had no stories to tell their children about Heaven. This policy of severely limiting access to Kabbalah and mysticism was reinforced in the nineteenth century by German Jewish scholars who wanted to suppress mysticism in order to portray Judaism as a rational religion. The religious training of most Conservative and Reform Jews, like Elinor, has been the product of this history.[3]

But in the 1920s, a young and brilliant Israeli scholar, Gershom Scholem, rebelled against tradition. He translated the entire Kabbalah from the ancient Hebrew into German. The last of Scholem's work was published in English just last year. A whole generation of rabbis is being exposed for the first time to mysticism and the idea of Heaven in the context of their religion's history. It is not just the rabbis who are learning. Workshops and conferences and night courses for laypeople have already been spawned. Sabbath school teachers can begin teaching the children. The curious of other faiths can pick up books on the subject at the local library or bookstore. What might Elinor have learned if she had sought out understanding of Jewish mysticism? One lesson in particular might startle her.

The Kabbalah teaches that specific changes occur at the moment of death. The physical body's energy dissolves. The transcendent part of the body, the *neshamah*, leaves and is greeted by the souls of others, often family members and friends, who died earlier. The *Zohar*, the main textbook of the Kabbalah, actually says: "For we have learned that at the hour of a man's departure from the world, his father and his relatives gather round him, and he sees them and recognizes them . . . and they accompany his soul to the place where it is to abide."[4]

Sound familiar? With no knowledge of the Kabbalah, and no sense that her religious tradition includes an afterlife, Elinor Finkelstein had a near-death experience that echoes almost exactly what the sacred texts of Judaism say will come to pass when she dies. Her father came. She saw him. The only difference is, he told her to go back. At the very least, Elinor could resolve that her near-death experience was not in conflict with her heritage. At a wider perspective, Elinor's experience is a source of religious revelation: it confirms a tenet of her religious heritage in a thoroughly modern way.

Naomi Rosen (not her real name) is a criminal lawyer with a large and demanding practice in Miami, Florida. She grew up in a Jewish household that emphasized the rational. Her mother's father was an Orthodox rabbi, but her father was very antireligious, so her parents compromised. They brought their children up in a Conservative congregation and emphasized politics. Heaven was never mentioned. As in Elinor's family, Naomi was taught that death is the end. There is no afterlife. Growing up, Naomi was taught that when you die, you deteriorate and become part of the earth. As she explains what she was taught, "The sense of the soul is whatever you have given to those around you."

A week after her twentieth birthday, Naomi went into the hospital for routine surgery for the removal of an ovarian cyst. Afterward, it was discovered that she had internal bleeding, so she was taken in for surgery again. In the recovery room, she developed a pulmonary embolism. She went into congestive heart failure.

"I had not yet regained consciousness from the anesthesia," remembers Naomi, "but I had a very vivid sense of what was happening. I had a sense of being suspended, that my body was suspended, and that I was outside my body, above my body, observing. I don't have a recollection of anything except my body and me. My sense was that my body was suspended but was being lowered, and that I knew that whenever it reached the bottom I would be dead. I was dying. It was very peaceful. Afterward that was what surprised me, how calm I felt about it all. So the experience is really one of being out of my body, and my body being lowered."

Some experiencers speak with awe. Some are filled with emotion, even twenty years after their experience. Naomi could have been in the courtroom, lawyer that she is, giving careful, point-by-point testimony: "During this experience there was a telephone that rang. And I knew the meaning of the telephone, and this was the meaning. When I was thirteen, we had a close family friend who had a son about a year older than I was. And he got the flu. Within a couple of days he died of spinal meningitis. The day or so that he was in the hospital my parents were there with his parents in the hospital. For much of the time, families rotated around the clock being with them. My parents had been at the hospital with Paul. Paul's parents had come home very late at night. At about two or three in the morning the phone rang, and I got it. The phone call was from other friends telling us that Paul had died.

"Well, in the experience, when the phone rang, I knew it was Paul. To me the phone ringing was Paul. It was Paul saying he was there. And that was the sum total of the experience. The experience was short, but it was powerful."

Naomi's perceptions of what happened were discounted at every turn: "When I told the doctors about it, they just sort of pooh-poohed it and said, 'When you had the embolism and went into heart failure, we put you on morphine right away. We wanted to keep you unconscious, and the morphine made you euphoric. That's what made you feel at peace.' Other people said, 'I bet there was a phone in the recovery room, and that could have been ringing.' There are explanations for different aspects—attempts to rationally explain different aspects."

But the attempts to explain her experience rationally did not satisfy Naomi. When asked how she felt about it, Naomi answered, "Very weird and very intrigued. I'd grown up in a very rational house, very Jewish, quite involved in being Jewish—celebrating holidays, learning the liturgy. But very rational. It was my first sense that [pause] maybe there is a world that we do not understand. And that maybe there really is something out there, a spiritual world that is just beyond my comprehension, and, until that point, beyond my experience. So it made me skeptical of my totally rationalist orientation toward the world. It didn't convince me that there is an afterlife, but it made me very open to the idea that there may be dimensions that I may not perceive."

Naomi connects her near-death experience to several aspects of her life since then. For months afterward she was uncharacteristically relaxed, simply grateful to be alive. She describes herself as "Miss Mellow" during that time. Her gratitude for the moment is a classic reaction to any close brush with death. But Naomi credits her NDE for this attitude, and there is some research evidence that she is right. In *Life at Death,* Dr. Kenneth Ring shows that after a brush with death, experiencers and nonexperiencers alike have the same pattern of positive attitude change. But there is suggestive evidence that, compared with nonexperiencers who have had a brush with death, experiencers have a greater appreciation of life. They are more apt to have a renewed sense of purpose and a feeling that they are stronger people.

Naomi is persuaded that the long-term effects in her case are a result of her near-death experience. Because she is by temperament a hardworking, even driven, person, she and her husband now keep Shabbat, that is, they do no work on the Sabbath. Says Naomi, "I think there is tremendous wisdom in the Sabbath, of giving yourself a day out of time. It is a way that I try to keep connected to whatever insight I gained. The experience was an out-of-time experience, the way Shabbat is an out-of-time day."

Naomi's children know about her experience. Having been terrified of dying since the age of eight, she is grateful to be able to tell her children that dying is a surprisingly peaceful and reassuring experience. She has found that several people who have life-threatening diseases have been drawn to her. She tells them her experience. "I'm basically not a touchy-feely type person, but there's just an openness that wouldn't have been there," says Naomi. She has toyed with the idea of going to rabbinical school.

Almost as an afterthought, Naomi added another salient feature of her life today. "I've just realized something I should mention that is so obviously relevant, I don't know why I didn't think of it. What I do is represent people on death row."

Naomi's voice had an intensity to it that had not registered before as she explained the circumstances of her law practice. "This is not what I started to do in law. I did it out of family needs. We found out after our first baby was born that he had chromosome damage, and he would be severely handicapped. He has actually done great . . . but two years later we had a second child, and realizing that the reality was that I had two babies, I had to give up the career track. So essentially I was looking around for something to do, and moaning and groaning about my situation, when a friend who is a criminal appellate lawyer offered me work.

"It was something I could keep my finger in. It was easy. At that time the courts were liberal, we won all our cases, no one ever got executed. Gradually over the years, I got more and more involved. Now I teach a course, I have cases of my own, it is very stressful. They execute people. I never thought of connecting it to my near-death experience, but I wonder."

Sammi Siegal was twenty-two years old and engaged to be married. She had been engaged to her fiancé, the younger brother of her sister's husband, on and off all through college. It was the spring of 1980. Her family owns a camping and sporting goods store. She and her fiancé were supposed to go down to Coconut Grove, Florida, to help her mother with a camping show, but Sammi insisted on going on a long bike ride. Sammi had been restless lately, feeling that she and her fiancé had not been doing as much athletically as they had been, and she missed it.

The day was glorious. It was during the years before bike helmets were required gear: Sammi was wearing a bathing suit and shorts and sandals. They had ridden their bicycles about seven miles, when Sammi was hit by a car. The impact of her body on the windshield smashed the glass. She was propelled 150 feet. Her face hit the pavement and she slid to a stop.

Sammi has no recall of the accident as it was just described. As she says, "My very first feeling was that I was dying and that it was wonderful. I could see bright yellows and whites and some sky blue kinds of colors, but it was mostly a blinding yellow brightness and it was a suction feeling, and I kept feeling as if I were moving farther and farther away. And I was thinking, 'If I'm dying, this isn't so bad.' Then I realized I had so much more to do in my life on earth. It was at that point that I went *vvvvpppp* [sic] right back."

Sammi explained that the moment of her transition into her body was not like a magician making someone levitate as she might have imagined. The moment felt more like a vacuum cleaner sucking her out.

Sammi had suffered a fractured skull and a concussion. She was in the hospital for a week. Rather than go on with a description of the physical consequences of the accident, Sammi proceeded to explain that, at the time of the accident, she had been doing her internship for her master's degree in music therapy with severely and mildly mentally disabled people. She felt that the acceptance of disability in the workplace made it possible for her to reenter the world after only six weeks at home. As she said, "It was easy to go back into a community where it just didn't matter to these people."

She mentioned casually that her leg was broken. Only then did

Sammi admit that the accident had left her with no teeth and no nose.

Her best friend came to see her in the hospital and said, 'Sorry, wrong room.' She had to call him back. When she went to shopping malls, children became frightened looking at her. Her own nieces and nephews did not want to kiss her because she had stitches all over her face. "They said I looked like Frankenstein," says Sammi now.

Sammi reported these reactions with a singular lack of self-pity or pain. She has had seven reconstructive surgeries. "It was about getting in touch with the me behind my face," she says. "A year later, I would forget about what I looked like on the outside. It was so clear to me that I am not about my skin. Or my nose. Or my teeth. Or my face. Or my eyes."

When asked if she would have known before the accident that her complete lack of self-pity or vanity would be her reaction, Sammi replied, "Oh, absolutely not. I was twenty-two. I cared about my weight, my looks."

No longer. As Sammi says, "In retrospect, because you ask me, vanity is such a phenomenally superficial concept. Once something so traumatic had happened in my life, it wasn't even a conscious thing. I am who I am behind my face."

Sammi broke her engagement to her fiancé. Before the accident, she had known in her heart of hearts that she did not want to marry him; her first thought when she regained consciousness was relief that she had not yet made the mistake of marrying. He was a nice man, but the wrong one for her. Her religious life changed dramatically. Sammi describes her parents as "clearly Jewish," but she herself had no religious training. Sammi Siegal's father had died of a heart attack when she was eleven. She remembers her mother saying at the time, 'Remember your father as he was, not as he is now.' Her mother became "very anti-God" after her father died. As Sammi describes her family, "The issue of soul and spirit were not part of the vocabulary of growing up."

As a teenager, Sammi had "dabbled" in religion, trying a youth group here and there, going to a few services at her university. It was not very satisfying. After her near-death experience, however, Sammi describes herself as being "on a mission." She married an Orthodox Jew whom she describes as very religious. "I wanted to be near him. I wanted to experience the singing of the language, Shabbat, the prayers, the liturgy. Shortly after I met him, I started studying the Torah and religion in general with a Lubavitch woman in Miami Beach. Her husband was the Lubavitch rabbi[5] of Miami Beach: a very, very spiritual person with a very large family. And it felt so comfortable. It felt as if I had gone home. It's really been since that point, for the last ten years, I've been on a deep spiritual quest."

Since her accident Sammi has earned her Ph.D. in music therapy and has become a professor with a joint appointment at the University of Windsor in Windsor, Canada, and Wayne State University in Detroit. Although she has since divorced her husband, she is raising her son with the religious values she has incorporated into her life since her NDE. She describes their home life as very observant. Her son goes to Hebrew day school. "I want my child to feel very close to God as he is growing up."

And what about death? Says Sammi quietly, "I know that my soul is eternal. I don't know if this is teaching or intuition, but I just know that I view my body and my soul as a horse and a rider. My body is just a physical carrier for my soul, which is eternal."

The Heaven of the Kabbalah, as in many other traditions, is often described as a spiritual region in which souls may continue to grow and learn, a dynamic place in which we can become ever closer to God. Mormons often depict Heaven this way, as do Muslims. A characteristic metaphor in the Jewish tradition is of a celestial academy. By the way Sammi described her intellectual and spiritual journey, it seemed that she would be comfortable with such a setting for the afterlife. Although the Kabbalah makes it very clear that such descriptions are not meant in a material sense, but as a state of awareness, there is an underlying sense in Judaism that the highest regions of the World to Come are most accessible to the spiritually educated.

But as in other traditions, Jewish mystics also wanted to make it clear that no one would be denied in the World to Come who had inner peace and knowledge, even uneducated Jews. There is a famous parable about an ignorant but devout coachman. He would have been unable to handle, nor would he have found happiness, in the highest regions of the World to Come where learned souls contemplate spiritual mysteries. So the "Heavenly Tribunal" sent him off to a world where he was given a magnificent carriage harnessed to four splendid horses. The roads stretched before him, dry and even and beautifully landscaped. As the sages explained, "Each man creates his own Paradise."[6] Even Jews who have had no religious training will have access to the World to Come.

It is moving, even cause for joy, that in this post-Holocaust time, more and more Jewish people may reclaim from their culture some sense that God's gifts extend past this life. A sophisticated Jewish man in his seventies, who has distinguished himself with his philanthropy, was weighing the evidence that Jewish near-death experiencers bring to bear on hope for the afterlife. He listened carefully and finally said what he thought. "It's too late for me," he said. "I'll never believe. I'm going to die and that'll be it. But maybe my kids will have hope."

NOTES

1. I hope that someone else in the field will do further study with a larger sampling of Jewish experiencers.

2. Genesis 28:16–17

3. To verify this startling fact, I called the top five rabbinical seminaries in the country and asked to speak to a presiding teacher of Jewish mysticism. Mysticism was taught only at the Orthodox schools.

4. *Zohar,* volume 2, p. 307.

5. Lubavitch is the name of one of many Hasidic dynasties that arose in the eighteenth and nineteenth centuries. It is now the largest in the world, with headquarters in Crown Heights, Brooklyn, New York. Sammi actually used the word *rebbe,* not *rabbi,* which is the Yiddish word for rabbi. However, some Jews feel that rebbe should be reserved for someone of Grand Master standing, so I have substituted the English word.

6. Hoffman, Edward, *The Way of Splendor,* p. 197.

Chapter 9

Who Has Been There Through the Ages and Come Back to Tell the Tale?

Behold, a sacred voice is calling you.
All over the sky a sacred voice is calling.

—BLACK ELK SPEAKS

The soldier of Er, as he was called, lay dead on a funeral pyre for twelve days. On the twelfth day he suddenly came back to life. He claimed that during the time he had lain on the funeral pyre, his soul had departed from his body and made a journey. He traveled to the gates of Heaven and hell.

The soldier of Er appears in the last chapter of Plato's *Republic*, written in the fourth century B.C.E. As Plato tells the story, the risen soldier reported that during his journey, he saw a panel of judges. When he himself came forward to be judged, the judges said that he had to become a messenger to human beings of all that he saw.

They told him to listen and to look at everything that was going on.

The soldier of Er saw openings to Heaven and earth from which souls were departing and returning. Those from Heaven told "of the inconceivable beauty of the experiences and the sights there."[1]

Plato was writing a philosophical tract, not a journalistic account. There is no way to assess whether there was a soldier of Er or if Plato reported his story accurately. But the soldier of Er's story has all the elements of a near-death experience. Death is established. The soul of the soldier makes a journey. Others are there to greet him, and he is given a judgment on his future. The gates of Heaven and hell act as a barrier. The soldier is given to understand that he must go back with a message for others. And so he comes back to life.

Although the notion of near-death experiences had not yet been introduced, the parallels between the story and NDEs are significant. Perhaps it is no accident that Plato was a powerful advocate throughout his writings for the existence of the soul.

He is also the first prominent thinker in the West who proposed a celestial Heaven. Myths and the writings of Homer suggest that ancient Greeks earlier than Plato believed in a murky underworld, a place called Hades that is perhaps best translated as "house of invisibility." Hades was a dreary place. Several Greek myths turn on human beings' attempts to trick their way out of the ghostly, dark abode of the dead.[2] A few heroes fare better than common folk. In the *Odyssey,* Homer has one hero going to the Elysian Fields and another to the Isles of the Blessed. The location of both these paradises seems to be somewhere on earth.

By the fifth century B.C.E., Orphic religious sects promised a blessed life after death. Pythagoras advanced a similar concept. But none made mention of the soul—the newly dead seemed to arrive in person. Plato, on the other hand, emphasized the idea that the soul could travel where the body could not to a heavenly abode. For example, in a gentle exchange between Socrates and Crito in the book of *Phaedo,* Plato illustrated his ideas about the soul traveling away from the body. The conversation occurs in Plato's account of Socrates' last visit with his friends before he drinks the deadly hemlock for his execution. Crito asks Socrates how they should bury him. "However you please," he replies, "if you can catch me and I do not get away from you."[3]

Socrates' response displays confidence that his soul will have left his body. His tone is playful. He is practically teasing Crito. Socrates—but remember that the writer here is Plato—is completely confident that the "I" of the dead body will have left the corpse for immortality.

Throughout his writings, Plato's arguments assume the separation of body and soul. The body, according to Plato, is simply a residence for the soul: sometimes a workshop, sometimes a prison. Although this idea may seem obvious to anyone acquainted with near-death experiences, Thomas Aquinas, a cornerstone thinker of Catholic theology, disagreed with Plato. He believed that body and soul could not be separated. That belief is hard to reconcile with an afterlife, unless it is paired with belief in bodily resurrection. Then again, Aquinas had an intense mystical experience a year before he died and repudiated his own thinking. His last written words were "Everything I have written is as so much straw."[4]

Ezekiel is an Old Testament figure who was given a lavish vision of Heaven. In the following excerpt, Ezekiel layers language, repeating himself, changing the description a little each time, as though he is trying to get it right. He evokes the colors of the rainbow just as Mary Dooley, the fashion designer, tried to describe colors. He even strings his sentences together with *ands,* a characteristic of every experiencer interviewed.

This is a difficult passage to understand. There is not much punctuation, and some of the language is old-fashioned. Reading it out loud may help. Said Ezekiel: "Above the firmament over their heads there was the likeness of a throne, in appearance like sapphire, and seated above the likeness of a throne was a likeness as it were of a human form. And upward from what had the appearance of his loins I saw as it were gleaming bronze, like the appearance of fire enclosed round about; and downward from what had the appearance of his loins I saw as it were the appearance of fire, and there was brightness round about him. Like the appearance of the bow that is in the cloud on the day of rain, so was the appearance of the brightness round about."[5]

In this passage, Ezekiel tries several different ways of describing the Light: "fire," "brightness," and "bronze." Most contemporary experiencers use "gold" and "golden" to describe the Light of their near-death experiences—but archaeological digs show that in Ezekiel's time bronze was used for mirrors and was a source of reflective light.

Ezekiel is one of the most important of the Old Testament prophets. Just after this vision, he was carried up into Heaven by chariot. The information he learned on his tour and was able to impart upon his return to earth is the basis of the Merkavah texts, the books of Jewish mysticism.

Dr. Carol Zaleski, professor at Smith College, has pointed out that the Bible includes near-death experiences as a source of mystical revelation. She has, for example, researched the story of Enoch. Enoch is a Biblical prophet who appears in the book of Genesis. The last of his lines is quite cryptic: "Enoch walked with God; then he was no more, because God took him."[6] According to Zaleski, apocalyptic writers filled in the details. In the oldest version of what happened, Enoch has a dream in which clouds and mist called to him, and stars and flashes of lightning provided the path on which winds lifted him up to Heaven. In the dream, Enoch faints. He is brought to a huge house of burning marble where he meets God face-to-face. He is then given a tour of Heaven that is both astrological—he is shown storehouses of stars, storms, and winds—and metaphysical. He is shown such secrets as where rebel angels are punished. The names of the good angels were revealed to him. Read as a near-death experience, Enoch's journey is quite similar to several contemporary accounts.

Mary Free, for instance, was given a tour of Heaven during her near-death experience. After receiving cosmic knowledge, she, like Enoch, saw what she calls the Creator's hands and head. Then she was allowed to look through a portal in His midsection to see more of the universe. Her view included a rosy pink planet with sandy orange rings. Diana Wood was also given a tour of the universe in which the Great Being, as she calls him, explained the nature of suffering.

There is substantial evidence that Saint Paul, one of the most influential New Testament figures, had a near-death experience. Nancy Evans Bush, president of IANDS and a student of the Bible, has speculated that Saint Paul may have had his near-death experience when he was stoned and left for dead in Lystra[7] or when he had his great revelation on the road to Damascus. The only thing the Bible says about his famous conversion is that as "he was going along approaching Damascus, suddenly a light from heaven flashed about him." A voice asked him why he was persecuting him. Saul asked who was talking to him. The voice answered that it was Jesus.[8] This is certainly not enough to stake a claim that Paul had a near-death experience. What lends support to that belief are his later writings. Paul confessed in Second Corinthians of having "visions and revelations of the Lord" that are strongly evocative of near-death experiences. Speaking about himself, he says: "I know a person in Christ who fourteen years ago was caught up to the third heaven—whether in the body or out of the body I do not know; God knows. And I know that such a person—whether in the body or out of the body I do not know; God knows—was caught up into Paradise and heard things that are not to be told, that no mortal is permitted to repeat."[9]

In this passage, Saint Paul repeats himself, much the way contemporary experiencers do when describing what they went through. He complains about the impossibility of explaining the experience in words. And he admits to the strong possibility of an out-of-body experience. He sounds rather like Linda Burnett, the atheist in Colorado who went to the end of a line of spherical lights leading to the glacier on Berthoud Pass during her near-death experience. She, too, was unsure of her form. She said, "All I can assume is that I must have been a sphere as well. I don't know that for a fact. But just at the point where, if I'd had a body . . ." As Saint Paul said, "Whether in the body or out of the body I do not know, God knows."

And then there is the transformation. As Linda went from atheism to a rich spiritual life, Saul went from persecuting Christians to becoming the figure we know today as Saint Paul. This is not to suggest that Linda is the same caliber of mystic. Near-death experiencers and the great mystics are united by a moment in common with the transcendent. But not every experiencer is a mystic. What separates them is the level of commitment to spiritual discipline—and willingness to testify publicly to what they have learned. Where Saint Paul understood himself to be called to bear witness to what he "knew," experiencers usually have only shared their experience with one, maybe two, confidants. But the similarities between modern-day experiencers and Saint Paul do suggest that a near-death experience may have been the source of religious revelation for Saint Paul.

Saint Paul a near-death experiencer! He wrote words any experiencer would agree with: "And now faith, hope, and love abide, these three; and the greatest of these is love."[10] Like experiencers, he completely lost any fear of death, and he had a powerful sense of mission. After the death of Jesus, Saint Paul and the other apostles spread the news of their conviction that Jesus had conquered death. Christians believe that, by faith, we participate in Jesus' victory. We will go to Heaven because he did.

The idea that Saint Paul was a near-death experiencer might perplex some people of faith. It is a common understanding among experiencers that their accounts often upset their ministers, rabbis, or priests. Dr. Raymond Moody has reported that clergy accuse him of selling "cheap grace." They may have a similar resistance to the notion that near-death experiences have informed religious mysticism through the ages. Why?

One of the mysteries of near-death experiences is the ways in which they support belief in some ultimate authority and the power of love, as most religions do, and yet don't specifically support doctrinal issues of any one religion.

There is strong feeling, going all the way back to Saint Augustine, that key to the Christian message are the reality and sting of death. If death is not painful but is instead the joyful transition that most experiencers say it is, the argument goes, then the resurrection has no meaning.

Ironically, it is Saint Paul himself who asked rhetorically the much-quoted line about the sting of death. In First Corinthians, he described to his readers the mystery of death. He said that we shall not sleep but be changed. Later in the same verse he went on to say that when human beings put on immortality,

> *then shall come to pass the saying that is written:*
> *Death has been swallowed up in victory.*
> *Where, O death, where is thy victory?*
> *Where O death, is thy sting?*[11]

Death is swallowed up in victory. Sounds just like something an experiencer would know.

It must be admitted that mystical experience, by its very nature, *should* be upsetting to anyone invested in religious dogma. Where dogma is historical and conservative, mysticism is rule breaking. Near-death experiences break the rules of common sense: you can't come back from death. They also tend not to conform to any one religious tradition. On both counts, they are understandably threatening to religious conservatism.

Perhaps it would be helpful to remind traditionalists that an "establishment" figure like Saint Paul was himself a rule breaker. Acts, the book of the Bible that tells of his ministry, frequently describes his being run out of town for his supposedly outrageous preaching. Moses, whose vision of the burning bush may also have been an experience of the Light,[12] preached directly against the worshiping of idols that was fashionable among his people. It is only over time that the mystical experiences of great religious leaders inform and transform the religious life of the worlds in which they occur, and become incorporated as religious dogma.

Evidence of near-death experiences can be found in other religious traditions, even if they are not explicitly identified as such. Black Elk, the remarkable Native American spiritual leader, had a near-death experience, although he lived before the term was introduced. Among Protestant visionaries, Jonathan Edwards of the Congregationalists had something extremely similar if not definitely a near-death experience, as did Joseph Smith of the Mormons, and George Fox, the founder of Quakerism. Many, many other religious traditions include death-related visions as a source of mystical information. The *Egyptian Book of the Dead* includes narratives that are strikingly similar to near-death experiences.

In the Islamic tradition, the prophet Muhammad learned

God's will and his role in that will through a visionary revelation that has similarities to a near-death experience. The simplest version of the story has Muhammad spending long periods in a cave on Mount Hira contemplating the will of God. After one extended stay in the cave, Muhammad felt himself enveloped by an overwhelming angelic presence. He resisted the presence out of sheer terror. Finally, after having been overwhelmed three times, Muhammad surrendered to the experience and found the first words of what was to become the Qur'an coming from his lips. He came out of a trance convinced that he was either supposed to preach or that he was mad. There was a strong tradition of *jinnis,* a sort of demon possession, in Arab culture, and Muhammad was terrified that he had been taken over. He ran from the cave, determined to throw himself over the cliff and kill himself. A voice called to him. He raised his head toward Heaven and saw the angel Gabriel, his feet astride the horizon, so overpowering that no matter where Muhammad looked, the angel was there. Muhammad returned home, trembling violently. His wife, the devoted Khadija, convinced him that whatever happened was an authentic religious experience; he was supposed to be a Messenger of God.

Muhammad had always believed that only a prophet of God could solve the many problems that existed in the Arab world. But as Karen Armstrong, author of *The History of God,* and others have pointed out, he had never imagined that he would be the one that could provide the vision. He was an ordinary man, a trader with little education, who was given divine knowledge and the directive to spread the word of God's love—just like contemporary near-death experiencers.

Whether or not Muhammad's heart stopped or his vital signs disappeared is, of course, impossible to determine. Several accounts of his revelation describe his vision enfolding him to the point of suffocation. What *is* certain from all the different accounts is that Muhammad had that overpowering sense of Spirit-filled reality that many experiencers share. He was transformed. His revelations continued. Although various Western biographers make a distinction between Muhammad's first call and subsequent revelations, Muhammad himself said in later years, "Never once did I receive a revelation without feeling that my soul was being torn away from me."[13]

Whatever the trigger for Muhammad's vision, it would be difficult to deny the striking resemblance to Ezekiel's vision in the sky and Saint Paul's revelation on the road. There is a pervasive likeness that builds a case for credibility.

It is common for researchers in the field of near-death studies to speak of the "early days" of the research as occurring in the 1970s. It is true that near-death experiences earned an organization, a journal, and even its name during this period. But as our light-filled tour through world religious history indicates, the experiences themselves have been shaping the spiritual lives of human beings ever since the written word was there to report them.

Plato, Saint Paul, Ezekiel, Muhammad: at first it seemed amazing that such key figures of spiritual history have reported visions so similar to near-death experiences. Nancy Evans Bush likens her discovery of near-death experiences in the Bible to growing up in a big old house. "You've always lived in the big old house," says Bush. "You know and love it and think you know every nook and cranny. And then you find out that the house is honeycombed with secret passageways. They have been there all along, but you never found them. And they are filled with light and treasures."

God speaks to us in the language we understand, but not necessarily within the rules of nature and neighborhood that we thought we could rely on. The Hebrew prophets called their experiences *kaddosh,* holiness, the terrifying otherness of God. Saint Paul was bewildered by what happened to him. "I do not know, God knows." Muhammad raced home to his wife with the plaintive cry "Cover me, cover me," to protect him from any more of Gabriel's presence. No wonder near-death experiencers, in the aftermath of their own glimpse of Heaven's light, take years to admit that something has happened. It should be some solace to experiencers, and inspiration to us, that they are in such good company.

NOTES

1. Plato, *The Republic,* edited by Alan Bloom, p. 298.
2. Sisyphus, for example, told his wife not to perform funeral rites on him so that he could trick the queen of the underworld, Persephone, into letting him return to life.
3. Quoted from Harold DeWolf's book *Eternal Life,* p. 20.
4. McInerny, Ralph. *St. Thomas Aquinas.*
5. Ezekiel 1:26–28. All the Biblical quotes with this one exception are from the New Revised Standard Version. The vision of Ezekiel is from the Revised Standard Version. In this instance I have decided to opt for the language of the older version because it is visually richer. Moreover, the New Revised Standard Version includes a key error. Four Hebrew characters that have traditionally been translated as "bronze" are translated inaccurately as "amber." The Revised Standard Version preserves the more accurate, traditional translation.

   I was first alerted to this passage by Nancy Evans Bush, president of the International Association of Near-Death Studies and a student of the Bible. The Old Testament is filled with near-death experiences. Besides Enoch and Ezekiel, she cites Jacob and Isaiah.
6. Genesis 5:24.
7. Acts 14:19–20.
8. Acts 9:3–6.

9. 2 Corinthians 12:1–4.

10. 1 Corinthians 13:13.

11. 1 Corinthians 15:54–55.

12. Steinmetz, Dov, M.D., "Moses' Revelation on Mount Horeb as a Near-Death Experience," *Journal of Near-Death Studies* 11, No. 4: 199–203.

13. Karen Armstrong, *The History of God*, p. 139.

Chapter 10

On Earth as It Is in Heaven: What Are the Aftereffects of NDEs?

What will the soul experience when it regains its senses and goes back to live in the world . . . ?

—SAINT TERESA OF AVILA, SIXTEENTH CENTURY

Your religion is where your love is.

—HENRY DAVID THOREAU

There is a story in Mahayana Buddhism of four wise men wandering in the desert. They came to a high wall, which the first man climbed. When he reached the top, he gave a yell of joy and jumped. The second and the third did the same. The fourth man, too, climbed to the top of the wall. He looked longingly at the gurgling stream, the trees laden with fruits, and the enchanting garden below him. But then he thought of all the other travelers still wandering in the parched desert. He jumped back down into the desert and set off to find other lost wayfarers to guide them toward the oasis. In the Buddhist tradition, the first three men were perfected disciples whose monumental concentration led them to Nirvana, where suffering and all stages of life are transcended. The fourth became a bodhisattva, one who chooses to postpone Nirvana to help others on the road to enlightenment.[1]

Near-death experiencers have climbed the high wall. They have glimpsed, in some profound, symbolic way, the spiritual garden on the other side. Medical circumstances and perhaps free will have determined that they return to the trials of this life. They are changed.

Much has been written about the changes that near-death experiencers go through, and with good reason. As Dr. Bruce Greyson, a psychiatrist and a leading researcher in the field, has pointed out, people can go through years of psychotherapy and display very little change; people who have had near-death experiences may go through radical personality shifts overnight. Aftereffects of near-death experiences, as author and experiencer Phyllis Atwater has remarked, are the yardstick by which the authenticity of near-death experiences can be judged.

In *Life After Life*, Dr. Raymond Moody proposed that experiencers become more focused on love and on learning as the point of life. They lose all fear of death. Other researchers have generally corroborated Moody's findings, while adding their own discoveries. In *Transformed by the Light*, Dr. Melvin Morse cites five long-term changes in experiencers: decreased anxiety about death, a greater zest for living, fewer psychosomatic symptoms, an increase in psychic abilities, and even higher intelligence. Dr. Kenneth Ring goes so far as to say in *Heading for Omega* that near-death experiencers may foreshadow a new age in consciousness.

One could get the impression, reading Morse and Ring, that near-death experiencers were some sort of spiritual Amazons. They seem to be more loving, more focused on lifelong learning,

and somehow wiser than mere mortals who have not been transformed by the Light. The reality is more subtle. In their unswerv-
ing belief in an afterlife and complete lack of fear of death, the
experiencers interviewed for this study absolutely reflect the findings of other studies. Their commitment to learning and to love is
also consistent with the findings of other studies. That commitment, however, seems to come with more emotional costs than
some other studies indicate. Furthermore, near-death experiences
act as an invitation to a spiritual journey that transforms how experiencers handle life's suffering.

After experiencers described the experience itself, they were
asked to describe their religious training growing up, and if their
religious beliefs had been affected by their experience. All knew
that they were being interviewed for a book about Heaven, which
could have biased their answers, so it was stressed that disbelief
was as interesting as belief. Most of the near-death experiencers
interviewed feel that they have changed spiritually because of
their experience and can point to their life situation to prove it.

Betty Jane Ramsey had a profound near-death experience in
which bells pealed, voices sang, and Jesus appeared in all his radiance. But just as Betty Jane reached out for Jesus, she began slipping back down.

"The bells stopped ringing and I became aware of people's
voices from the waiting room," said Betty Jane. "I could feel the
cold, hard tile on the floor where I was lying."

In a follow-up interview, Betty Jane explained that at the time
of her near-death experience, she was married with two daughters, ages one and two. She had finished high school but had no career aspirations or desire to go to college. She had always been
timid. As she said, "Everything was wonderful at home. I really
didn't know in what direction my life would go."

When it was pointed out that she must have had her hands full with a one- and two-year-old, she replied, "I know, that's what's so strange about this. I went back to college and I finished. I would get up at six to go to work in a plant until four, then go to class until ten o'clock at night, then read until two o'clock in the morning, and then get back up at six and go to work. And I did this for three and a half years. I finished four years of college in three and a half years. I took care of two kids and the house and everything in the meantime. Looking back now, I don't know how I did it. And I have continued my education. It's like I have to. I don't know why I have to . . . I never would have gone to college if it hadn't been for my experience."

Betty Jane's response to her experience is a classic aftereffect: the pursuit of knowledge. She became a schoolteacher who has taught for the past seventeen years. There was a considerable cost. Betty Jane went back to school on the regimen just described when her youngest daughter started kindergarten. She feels that she "missed out" on three years of her youngest daughter's life. While she is close to her daughter now, she wonders if her daughter's rebelliousness during her teenage years, including time taken out from schooling, was linked to Betty Jane's drive for education. Mostly there is a gnawing feeling that she missed a precious time of her daughter's development.

Betty Jane was brought up Missionary Baptist. Her church "makes a big issue" of going to church every week. She now gets the feeling that the church has a philosophy that God is only at church. She says she was brought up to believe that "you work six days a week, and then on Sunday you go to church. And that's what's going to get you into Heaven."

Whereas Betty Jane used to go to church several times a week, she now does not go even once a week regularly. "I just don't have that feeling anymore that church is the only place where God is. I have this feeling that God is everywhere. I don't care where I go.

If I go to South America, if I go down in the ravine, if I go to the creek, if I go to the tallest mountain, if it's night, if it's day, whatever, I feel that God is there with me."

Again, her change of heart about church had its cost. It is awkward for her marriage, as her husband is still deeply involved in the church. Statistically, however, she has been lucky to hold on to her marriage. Many experiencers find that their relationships cannot absorb the changes near-death experiences bring. Although experiencers say that they are more focused on love since their NDE, the divorce rate among experiencers is slightly higher than the national average.

Some experiencers say a new clarity about love demands the sloughing off of stunted relationships. Others find their relationships deepen. But it is in experiencers' attitude toward themselves where the lesson of love has resonated most profoundly. No matter what their station in life, level of education, or accomplishment, experiencers are grounded in self-acceptance. Having felt ineffable love during their near-death experiences, they convey a sense of believing absolutely in the value of their own lives.

Mary Pollak is a thin, intense woman in her late thirties who went through dramatic relationship changes because of her near-death experience. She is a legal secretary who specializes in divorce law. The birth of her first two children had been uneventful. But when she arrived at the hospital to give birth to her third child, the baby was running out of fluid. She was put under general anesthesia for an emergency cesarean section.

According to Mary, she started to float. She passed the room her husband was in. He was walking around. She said to him, "This is what it's like to die. I'm okay, don't worry about me." He did not hear her. As she remembers what happened next, "I went farther along, and I came into a space that was at a different level, a different height. This is hard to explain . . . bear with me. I got

into this space, and I was met by two people that I had known."
One was her father, who had died five years earlier.[2]

"I smiled at them and they smiled at me, and I get chills every
time I talk about it. This wonderful greeting. I said some word,
some sound that meant 'What am I doing here?' and when I said
it, I got a flood of knowledge. I looked at them and knew why I
was there. It was all telepathic, no verbal communication. [I said]
you mean that's all I had to do was say this password and I had the
answers to every question? And they smiled and said, 'It was
nothing we could teach you. You had to learn it for yourself.'
They left and I became flooded with the Light. I started then
being surrounded by a white light. I had total and complete
knowledge of everything there was to know about everything.
Everything made sense. There was no more mystery. I became
where I was. I became the Light, and the knowledge and the wisdom. Complete and absolute love. All love. And I was embraced
by it, and held by it, and it was blissful. I don't know how long I
was there. There was no time and there was no space. It was just
being in the Light. The love was so intense. I was everything I
was *feeling*.

"The next thing I knew I was coming down. And I was coming down in a very deep tunnel. Headfirst, very very fast, rapid
speed. And everything I knew was slipping away from me. Like it
was going backwards. And it was very loud and clamorous and
dark. All the voices I had ever heard, all the words in the universe,
and everything I knew was happening at the same time. And it
was like a mumble jumble of different languages, different
tongues being spoken. Very loud and bangy and clangy.

"I thought I was screaming and it was so painful and I came
out! And I woke up. I looked around and my husband was holding
our baby at the bottom of the bed. And my first conscious thought
was, Who was born here? I thought I was born. I didn't know
what this was."

The next day, she tried to tell her husband what had happened. She said, "I've discovered the secret of life."

He thought she was "nuts." So she kept quiet about it and read everything she could find that might explain what had happened to her. It was not an easy time. Says Mary, "Luckily I remembered going to a psychic on a lark with a girlfriend, and the psychic's husband said then that she didn't used to have this power until she almost died once."

Mary tracked down the woman. The woman told her that her husband had been referring to her experience. Mary had never heard of NDEs, so she felt even more peculiar. But then her sister found the International Association of Near-Death Studies (IANDS). Says Mary now, "For the first time in a year and a half, I knew I wasn't crazy."

Mary was raised a Catholic, but she found that because of her near-death experience, she did not want her baby son christened: "The spiritual was not to be confined to religion. I didn't want my son locked into the rules and regulations. I believe our God is the inner voice inside that tells us which way to go and what to do and not to do. That God is complete and absolute love."

Like Betty Jane, Mary was kicked out of the easy Eden of her church's teachings when she had her near-death experience. This does not mean that her religious life is over. She takes very seriously negotiating with her son's father what kind of religious training her son will have. She also realized that she had a new-found spiritual responsibility to herself.

Change was awkward. At a barbecue or some other casual social gathering, Mary would start talking about God's love. People would look at her with perplexed expressions and drift away. She found that she could not drink alcohol anymore. She "went cold turkey."

Looking back, Mary says she had been an alcoholic. By forgoing drink, she upset the rules of her marriage. She says, "My husband would sit there on Sunday with a beer watching TV and I'd sit there watching him watch TV. After the experience, that wasn't satisfactory anymore. I couldn't waste any more time . . . I had something to do here."

She got herself into a twelve-step program of Alcoholics Anonymous for five years. Her commitment to stop drinking broke up her marriage. But there were benefits, too. As Mary says, "I had something to do here. I don't exactly know what that is yet, except help people. I sponsor three people in the program (Alcoholics Anonymous). I'm a much better mother. I wasn't abusive, but negligent. Now I'm involved. It's like one thing led to another. Alcoholism was all through my family. And I wouldn't have faced it if it weren't for the experience. I feel blessed."

Mary believes that her experience has changed her children, her sister-in-law, and "the ten people who tell it to the next person." She shares her story whenever she can with people going through grief.

Mary's convictions about love emerge in three different areas of her life. First there is the self-love that propelled her into the twelve-step program. Then there was the radical change in her attitude toward being a parent. Soon after her experience, she started requiring her older daughter and son to do their homework at a set time and to show her their work when they were done. One of her teenagers, a listless student, pleaded with her to "go back to the way she had been before that experience of hers." But the daughter's performance in school turned around. Then there is the love that compels Mary to help others in AA and overcomes her shyness in telling others who are grieving what she has learned about death.

There is no way to compare objectively Mary's self-concept after her near-death experience with her sense of herself before it. We do know that before her experience, she was an alcoholic in a parched marriage who did not, by her own description, give as much to her children as she should have. None of these attributes speak of someone with high self-esteem. But notice how she describes herself now: "I had something to do here"; "I'm a much better mother"; "I feel blessed"; "I think I'll be really happy." Mary learned self-love in her near-death experience.

There is nothing romantic about the love Mary now advocates. Love is hard work. Giving up alcohol takes constant vigilance. Letting go of a bad marriage is painful no matter how justified. Becoming an involved mother takes time and a willingness to be unpopular with one's children.

Other experiencers, too, have found that the requirements of the love they learn about in their near-death experience are challenging. Gail McKechnie is a white Zimbabean, currently living in northern Italy who has lived all over the world because of her husband's work as an executive for an oil company. Their constant moving necessitated Gail's giving up her own career aspirations. She had her two sons young. In 1984, when her youngest son was eight, Gail contracted cerebral malaria.

Gail was in the second cycle of the malarial attack, semidelirious with fever, when she could feel herself floating away. She says her NDE was like traveling inside a ridged drinking straw. "It was a bit womblike," remembers Gail. "It was like sitting on the edge of a warm pool. I was headed down the void, weightless. It wasn't exactly floating. It was like swimming down the void."

Gail had gone on "several little trips" into the void during her fevers. "The time I let myself go, I got tired of hanging on—it was so nice. I had a feeling of lightness and peace and restful feeling. I realized that if I went to the other side, I wouldn't be able to come back. I got scared, petrified. I had two small children. And I was scared because of my upbringing, the hellfire and damnation they taught. It took a long time to connect to my body because I had a yearning to go back."

Gail believes that one of the biggest changes for her was in her tolerance of other people's shortcomings. In particular it changed her relationship to her eight-year-old. She had been eager to get going on a career and had been seeing her youngest as an impediment to her aspirations. As she says now, "I loved Andrew, but I didn't always like him. He was so sweet, but he wanted me to play a role I didn't want. He wanted me to be his mummy. I didn't want to. I was resisting it."

Her near-death experience changed her attitude. "After my NDE, I realized I had to get to know him. I had to solve *my* problem with Andrew. We spent a lot of time together. I understood his need. We managed to work it out."

The payoff for Gail of a commitment to love is a wonderful son. Her relationship with Andrew, now eighteen, is easygoing and affectionate. But the hard work of that commitment goes on. Her decision to forgo a career has had its costs. Her boys no longer live at home. Her husband has retired early. Still elegant and slim, not yet fifty, Gail seemed restless. Whether or not a career would have changed how she feels about her life now is only speculation. She is resigned to her life.

Warren Doe chose to come back into his "mangled mess" of a body after a suicide attempt because he became convinced during his near-death experience that even in a coma, life was a precious gift. One year after his NDE, Warren became engaged. His fiancée discovered from the routine blood tests given when they applied for the marriage license that she had lupus.

By any standard, a diagnosis of terminal illness in oneself or someone beloved is one of life's most painful challenges. Yet Warren had no feelings of wanting to escape, nor did he feel bitter. Quite the contrary. Warren described his wife as an example of the ways in which his near-death experience had come true. During Warren's NDE, his "angel attorney" told him that life has purpose. Says Warren, "He told me, 'You made the right decision" [to return to life] because you're important to the scheme of things. You will do something that is very important."

Warren speaks with considerable energy and pride about the way he nursed his wife. He talks about sitting her on the porch on sunny days after various stints in the hospital. He describes staying in her hospital room day after day teaching the nurses that her coma was a stage of life to be learned from. He taught the nurses how to "read" her physical signs—that a twitch of a cheek, or a blink of an eye was her way of communicating, and that he could act as translator. By careful observation, Warren learned when his wife was asking for more morphine, and even more significantly, when she was asking for less. He feels joy that she died with no morphine in her system, comfortable and also aware for what he called "her transition to the other side." He describes himself as a guide in her journey toward the Light.

Anne McAvoy conveys the same sense of joy in the midst of suffering. She had her near-death experience in 1951, during a nine-hour operation for a brain tumor. She came out of the anesthesia, aware of a lot of people in the operating room. The chaplain was there. She could hear him "intoning Latin." He was giving her last rites.

As Anne tells her story, she could "feel her spirit leaving her body. It was almost a physical feeling." She felt it leaving at the thorax at the base of the throat, instead of from the top of the head as she has heard most people do. She thought to herself, "Well! Look at this!"

As Anne remembers what happened next, her surroundings became "incredibly dark. It wasn't a tunnel. There was no edge to it. It was more like infinity. I was going at a tremendous speed.

I've heard it described as the speed of light, but it felt as if it must be the speed of thought. Incredibly fast. I did not see a light at the end of it, but I came out of it into, well, I don't know whether to call it a void or not. It was a place with no light at all and no darkness at all. It was totally colorless and it was infinite. I have a feeling that there was more toward somewhere, but not where I was. There was just incredible energy, vast, infinite energy. Very strong.

"At the same time there was a feeling of great comfort and serenity and love. And I had the feeling that finally I had come home. After all these years of wandering, you know." She chuckled. "I wanted to stay there more than I have ever wanted anything in my life. I thought I'd like to mingle with this energy in some way, in whatever way it happens. I didn't care whether I lost my identity or whatever the story was, as long as I could be part of it.

"And then, I don't know how long I was there, could have been minutes, could have been seconds, could have been who knows, when all of a sudden I thought, 'Ohh, what about Harry?' I was newly married, only about eight months. And of course the minute I thought, 'I had a brain to think with,' and I was back in my body. But I was angry. I didn't want to be back in my body, but there I was.

"And that's about the size of it, except for one other thing. When I was out there on the edge of that energy vastness, I had a very acute awareness of everything that had ever happened, everything that was happening, or everything that would happen. And I had the feeling that all I had to do is zero in on anything and I'd really know it in detail. I didn't do that, but I felt that I could. And later I thought, 'Gee, this is what God does, but I'm not God.' Nevertheless, that was the way it was."

Anne went into a coma. Her doctor said later it was the most discouraging operation he had ever performed. He had not had much hope for her recovery. Afterward she asked the chaplain to come see her. She told him what had happened. According to Anne, he looked at her as if to say, "'You poor hallucinatory creature, you.' So I gave that up."

The year was 1951, twenty-four years before Raymond Moody would publish *Life after Life*. After the encounter with the chaplain, she only told her mother and a close friend. She doesn't think either of them believed her. Later she told a friend who was dying, and that friend did not believe her either.

According to Anne, she had a hard time just surviving the next five or six years. She was "quite disabled," with some paralysis in her face, and other weaknesses that did not show, like poor balance, weakness on her left side, and loss of hearing in one ear. Henry turned out to be an alcoholic. She divorced him within two years. It was hard to get a job with the facial paralysis.

When asked how her morale had fared during these difficult years, she answered, "Oh, fine. Couldn't have been better. I knew that I had been close to God."

Religious training had not been part of Anne's upbringing. She had gone sporadically to Sunday school in a Protestant church from ages eight to ten "and didn't get anything out of it." Anne's sense is that the church frowns on these experiences. "They want us to believe that the only avenue to God is through them. If that's what they want to believe, that's their business. That's their problem."

She admitted, laughing at herself, that for many years she thought she must be extraordinary because she had been so close to God. It was a relief, but also humorous to Anne when the first Gallup poll came out about near-death experiences in the early 1980s. Anne discovered that one in twenty Americans has had an experience similar to hers.

By her own assessment, Anne became a much more spiritual person after her near-death experience. "Instead of thinking in concrete terms—'What can I do that will be good for me?'—I started to think in abstract terms. I think a lot about the course of humanity over the last ten million years, how it has grown, and where it is headed. And how to make people feel better. I don't go around being a little ray of sunshine all the time, but if anyone gives me a lead, I pick it up."

Her voice became charged with energy when asked if she had changed in any way because of her experience. "Oh, indeed I did. I did a 180-degree turn. In almost everything. In all my values. My Henry was very conservative, and my parents were quite strict. And I was not a nice person. I didn't even like myself very well."

She says she had always excused herself. "Oh, I'm not such a bad person. But I was a very bad person. I did wrong things all the time. I was very destructive, and I was nasty if people didn't play the way I wanted to play. So I had very few friends. But after I came out of this, all of a sudden, without even trying, I liked other people. And so without even trying, I had loads of friends. So it made a great deal of difference in my life."

It is hard to imagine Anne being nasty or having few friends. At the annual conference of the International Association of Near-Death Studies, people kept coming up to greet and hug her, an elderly woman leaning on a cane. She has a wonderful laugh.

Anne became an arts-and-crafts teacher after her experience. She first worked in a hospital and later in a nursing home. She believes that her patients trusted her because of her facial paralysis.

When asked about other changes resulting from her experience, she said, "Well, money no longer meant a particle to me. With the facial paralysis making it hard to get a job, she was "very very poor for a very long time," but it didn't bother her.[3]

It would be natural to assume that life comes more easily to near-death experiencers than it does to the rest of us. If they were lucky enough, and maybe their luck meant good enough, to feel they had sure knowledge of Heaven, then they must have good and lucky lives.

As Warren and Anne can attest, this notion is wrong. First, there are the circumstances that contributed to the near-death experience, causes ranging from car accidents to abuse, rapes, and attempted murder, to heart disease and suicide. Many experiencers require long periods of recuperation. Chronic pain or disfiguration plagues some. And there are the consequences of being near death: jobs lost, loved ones mystified and suspicious of the stories experiencers tell, dreams smashed.

Yet Anne does not moan about her facial paralysis. If anything, she believes her patients trust her more because of her affliction. Besides being radically self-affirming, Anne's attitude reflects one of Christianity's most difficult-to-follow injunctions on suffering. In Romans 8:28, Saint Paul says, "We know that all things work together for good for those who love God, who are called according to his purpose."

Think of Laurelynn, for whom a botched medical procedure has meant seven operations, constant physical problems, the death of a promising career as a tennis professional, and uncertainty over whether she can bear children. She admits that there have been times when she "would really welcome death." But, like Warren and Anne, there isn't a trace of bitterness in her. Her face seems lit from an inner lamp when she smiles, and in a group she is constantly affirming of other people. At a recent meeting for near-death experiencers she confided that she has now accepted that God had other plans for her than tennis. Now a massage therapist, she said, "As I learn how to heal myself, I can be a model for others." No self-pity. Like Warren with his dying wife, Laurelynn has transformed her suffering into a life mission.

This is not to say that Laurelynn or any of the other experiencers are gunning for sainthood. Near-death experiencers struggle just as much as the rest of us with life's challenges. They, too, sometimes fail. After divorcing Henry, Anne married and divorced yet another alcoholic. After his wife's death, Warren got involved with a male high-school student whom he taught, for which he was sent to jail for two years. The difference is that experiencers see life's difficulties and suffering as a lesson. Their near-death experience does not guarantee that they have arrived spiritually. Rather, their experience acts as an invitation to begin a spiritual journey.

Consider, for example, experiencers' relationship to church. Agnostic experiencers who were not church attendees prior to their experiences tend to join a church or a synagogue afterward. Betty Jane, Mary, and Anne, who had been churchgoers before their experiences, all seemed to outgrow church in favor of more self-directed and universalist beliefs. There seem to be stages of spiritual development. A near-death experience tends to move an experiencer on to the next one.[4]

For Charlene Groves, her near-death experience has been a source of strength and joy in the midst of lifelong suffering. She was no stranger to hardship. She was brought up in a large family during the Depression. Her father was out of work. Her parents had met in a Presbyterian youth group, but when her father begged for work in exchange for food at their Presbyterian church, the church turned him down. Charlene ascribes his subsequent alcoholism to his misfortunes.

Charlene speaks with anger about the few times she went to Sunday School. "We colored pictures and sang simple songs—but it bored me. I wanted to know some answers about life. I was already so unhappy. I needed something I wasn't getting. Stories like Jonah and the whale had no meaning for me. No one interpreted them. I was supposed to take them literally. A fish swallowed a man. I could not relate it to my life. I could not relate religion to everyday life."

After Charlene was raped and strangled, she talked to the hospital psychiatrist. He was not helpful. The fifties were sexist, Freudian times. Her psychiatrist actually asked her if she had enjoyed it. He made the comment "Well, we all know how you airline hostesses are. You hang around in bars and pick up men."

The lack of support went from bad to worse. Before he left, Charlene's attacker told her that he would find her again, a comment that was published in the newspaper account of her ordeal. The other "career girls" who shared an apartment with her fled before she came home from the hospital. It was raining the night she returned by taxi to the deserted apartment. She stood on the porch, drenched and terrified that the rapist was stalking her, crying as she fumbled for her key.

A woman came out of a house across the street. Her apartment mates had "warned" Charlene about that house. People who were "weird," "not like us," and of various skin colors were always going in and out, they said. But the woman had read the newspaper account and spoke kindly to Charlene, saying she shouldn't have to be by herself. Charlene accepted the woman's invitation to spend the night. As it turned out, the house was a center for people of the Baha'i faith. Baha'is believe that all religions are essentially one. Charlene's religious education began that evening.

Three months after the rape, Charlene was on a plane that ran into trouble. In the midst of a snowstorm, the airplane suddenly dropped 1,000 feet. The plane was iced over. The lights went out. One of the passengers panicked. Recalls Charlene: "I got up to help the woman, who was going out of her mind from fear. I never should have gotten out of my seat, but she was terrifying the other passengers, who were already scared. Someone had placed a typewriter in the overhead rack. The typewriter flew out and hit me in the back."

As a result, Charlene has lived with chronic pain for the last forty years. An operation in 1972 was not a success.

What does all this suffering have to do with the aftereffects of near-death experiences creating Heaven on earth? Everything. Most of us think of Heaven on earth as those moments when we are surrounded by good friends or loving family sharing a happy moment. But near-death experiencers know differently. Heaven on earth are those times when we accept our fate and are able to celebrate the goodness of life in spite of the suffering we must bear.

At first, Charlene did not know what to think of her near-death experience, having never heard of such a thing. But then she picked up Raymond Moody's book in a secondhand bookstore. Now Charlene speaks of her experience as a source of strength. As she said, "Once I had that experience, I knew there was something to religion, but that it was more than taking some story literally—and more than something that only existed once, two thousand years ago, for three years and that was it. So from then on I constantly searched to know more about spirituality."

Charlene's near-death experience acted as an invitation to a spiritual journey. "It sent me on, year after year, seeking and reading about religion and the spiritual life. My search brought happiness into my life. Moments of real heightened pleasure and joy and awe. I had a thirst for knowledge that could not be satisfied. The more I read about religion, the more I read about holiness and spirituality. I want to know everything."

Whereas she never got much out of Bible stories as a child, Charlene spoke at length about Job, the quintessential Biblical sufferer. Her identification with him is a source of solace.

Charlene's "pleasure and joy and awe" in the midst of a life of so much pain is testimony to the power of near-death experiences. The commitment to affirm life's goodness, even in the face of suffering, points to the religious meaning of near-death experiences. In the aftereffects, experiencers are acting on earth as it is in Heaven.

Almost all experiencers speak with complete certainty that they will participate in an afterlife. Several national studies propose that 98 percent of all experiencers believe in an afterlife; the experiencers interviewed for this study concur. It is the only aftereffect for which there is such a remarkable degree of consensus.

Sally Pearce was thirty-three when she entered the hospital for day surgery for an ephemeral hernia. It turned out to be an enlarged and very infected lymph gland. According to Sally, during the surgery the infection in the lymph gland "got loose."

Sally heard the nurse say, "She is going sour. What do we do now?"

Sally was in searing pain. She says, "I literally thought the bed was on fire. They got me onto a respirator and IVs. I realized I was looking at them and my body from off the foot of my bed up in the air rather than from inside my head. I watched them rushing around and hooking me up to all these things. Then I went completely out of there. I wasn't in that room or in that place in any way. I was wherever. I didn't really know. I wasn't frightened; I was curious.

"I became aware shortly after that that I wasn't by myself. It's very hard to talk about where you were and what it looked like and what it felt like. Because it's so different, you can't describe it in earthly terms. For me, the sense of someone being there next to me was the important thing.

"I had been in some pain from the surgery. When I woke up, I literally thought the bed was on fire. I didn't even have to talk or listen. Whatever I felt was communicated, and things came back.

It became clear pretty quickly that it was God I was talking to. I have never changed from that opinion in all the years since. I kept thinking this was pretty nice because I did have an overwhelming sense of being loved and cherished. And I had no more pain. And I thought, 'Gee, this is great'"—Sally started to chuckle—"'but I have tiny children. I can't stay here. I have to go back and take care of my children.' I just thought that and what came back to me was 'Whatever you think you need to do, you'll do.'

"So very shortly after that I woke up in my body, and I don't know what time it was. Things like time and space and speech and hearing don't mean anything. They don't work that way."

Sally attended a Congregational church growing up and sang in the choir. She does not attend regularly now. She says, "The basic thing that changed is that now I know the things people say but don't really believe: God is love. There is nothing exclusive about God whatsoever."

Sally mentioned listening to a priest giving a lecture about death in which he quoted Jesus saying "I am the Way." She said she "had no problem with that—he is as good a way as any to get to God and to get to Heaven." When he said that Jesus was the only way, however, she has "a big argument with that. I clearly believe that everybody goes there. There's no such thing as hell or purgatory. God's love is truly unconditional."[5]

Unlike many experiencers, Sally feels sure that when she dies it will be a similar experience to her first time. Her conviction makes her an advocate for not prolonging dying. She frequently says in her talks and to doctors whom she meets, "Let it happen. Get out of the way." As Sally says to whoever asks, "I have absolutely no fear of death whatsoever."

Gail McKechnie had been terribly afraid of death because of her religious upbringing in a repressive girls' school in Zimbabwe. She was constantly threatened with hellfire and damnation. She thinks it may be impossible to communicate how liberating death actually is. "I enjoyed feeling the freedom of death," says Gail now. "I wish I could describe it. But not being afraid of dying is like saying riding a bicycle is easy. Until you've done it yourself, you don't know."

Asked how she felt about death, Betty Jane Ramsey paused in reflection. "I think I'm looking forward to it," she finally said with a laugh. Betty Jane is only forty-four and in good health. When asked what she is looking forward to in death, she answered, "I don't know—the richness of it, the peace, the joy, but I think it would be just a beautiful experience. From then on."

When asked what she thought was going to happen when she died, Mary Pollak's voice filled with cheer, as though talking about a reunion, or an outstanding party. Before her near-death experience, she always thought of Heaven as the chance to see her father and grandparents, and "just hang out for eternity." Now she sees it as a passage into the next stage of her soul's growth, a continuation of love and knowledge and service. "I think I'm going to be really happy. When I die, I'll be met by people I know who have been dead. I think I'll rest for a while, and I'll see some people I know. And then I'll help others come over. I'll be there to meet them."

Lehman Woods, the executive at the computer technology company, said that he wasn't sure that he was going to die. He thinks we just change. "I mean, I've been dead. Physical existence as we know it does, in fact, cease. I would consider it a liberating event. The body is a magnificent piece of machinery, but it is just that, a machinery that is occupied by a being who brings it life. And when the car wears out, you get another one . . . Your existence changes and your knowledge of yourself changes. But I don't think you die."

When Anne McAvoy was asked if she were scared of dying,

she said, "No, good heavens no. I'll welcome it. It's a good place to be." She hopes she'll go back to the place where she went during the NDE. She also hopes to go beyond that, as she says, "not just because other people have experienced bright lights and all that, that's other people. I just felt there was more to it. But this was great, I didn't care if I melted and became that energy.

"I'm seventy-eight, and the closer I get to the edge, the better I like it. But I don't want to go now, I have too much to do. I'm hoping to do some hospice work, because people are so afraid of dying."

Agnostics and critics of belief in Heaven are apt to see faith as a crutch. They believe that concern with Heaven is just a way to avoid the problems of this life. The reactions of near-death experiencers to their glimpse of Heaven's light mitigate these concerns. The experiencers use their knowledge of the afterlife to change how they live their lives now. They are ordinary people who have faced the problems of this life in new and radical ways because of near-death experiences. Some, like Laurelynn or Warren, go into healing professions or see the nursing of loved ones as the purpose of their lives. Some, like Betty Jane and Sally, are driven to learn or to teach. For others, the change is more inward. Mary stopped drinking; Anne changed the quality of her relationships. Each used the lessons of a near-death experience to affirm life. They have accepted the invitation to a spiritual journey and a life committed to love and learning. These aftereffects are the true proof that near-death experiences are authentic. What science cannot confirm, the hearts and actions of experiencers bear witness to.

Imagine, for a moment, the bodhisattva setting off into the desert after he chose to postpone Paradise. He looks purposeful as he trudges through the scorched terrain. Having seen his glorious destination, he now views his personal difficulty in the desert as a passing thing. His choice, although on the surface self-sacrificing, creates opportunities. He has the strength to endure all things, learn life's lessons, and to open his heart to others.

—————

NOTES

1. Huston Smith, *The Religions of Man,* pp. 184–185. This story comes from the Mahayana tradition, which has a rich cosmology of heavens, hells, and descriptions of Nirvana. Theravada Buddhism tends to be more reticent.

2. Mary believes that the other person was her lover who was stationed at the time on a ship at sea. Dr. Bruce Greyson, head of research for the International Association of Near-Death Studies, knows of no other near-death experience in which a person *currently alive* was cited.

3. I wish I had asked all my experiencers about money. In his book about aftereffects, *Transformed by the Light,* Dr. Melvin Morse has found that experiencers become less materialistic; I realized too late in my research that such an aftereffect is part of one's spiritual growth. I can say anecdotally that many of my group spoke spontaneously and persuasively of their lack of interest in wealth. See *Transformed by the Light* by Cherie Sutherland for more on this subject.

4. Compare James W. Fowler's *The Stages of Faith.*

5. Notice that this attitude contradicts the beliefs of experiencers in previous chapters.

Chapter 11

The Case for Heaven

For nothing worthe proving can be proven
Nor yet disproven: wherefore thou be wise,
Cleave ever to the sunnier side of Doubt.

—ALFRED, LORD TENNYSON
THE ANCIENT SAGE

Jonah did not want to go to Nineveh, as God bid him, to warn the inhabitants of that decadent city that they should change their ways. So Jonah skipped town. He headed by boat to the city of Tarshish. God sent a huge wind. When the crew of the boat figured out Jonah was the cause, they hurled him in the deep. He sank into the sea and became lunch for a whale.

After three days in the reeking interior of the fish, Jonah offered God a prayer, remarkable for its lack of self-pity. "Out of the belly of Sheol [the dwelling place of the dead] I cried," says Jonah, "and thou didst hear my voice . . ."

I went down to the land
whose bars closed upon me forever;
yet you brought up my life from the Pit.[1]

Jonah was thanking God for delivering him from death, without a word of complaint about his current, dark situation. So the Lord spoke to the whale, who obediently coughed up Jonah onto dry land.

Almost all of us at some point in our lives have descended into the dark of having our hearts broken. Disease, loneliness, failure, or loss has thrown us into the belly of a metaphorical whale. Surely this is true for experiencers. Think of Charlene Groves. The child of a dysfunctional family, raped and strangled at twenty-two, she has endured more than forty years of severe physical pain from a work injury. Listening to her story, one wishes there were some way to rescue her from her life.

But there is no need. She has already been rescued. Charlene—and all the experiencers—have been grabbed by grace. They were yanked into the Presence of radical love and taught that their spirits will continue in that love after they die.

Most of us are not so lucky. Doubt can surround us like a clammy fog, and it isn't clear that the Light will ever get through.

For those who aren't experiencers, believing in Heaven is a journey, and we all haul the weight of our collective doubts. Politics, science, psychology, and our personal histories have contributed to a culture of doubt. But near-death experiences create a new culture. They give us the evidence needed to make a decision about Heaven.

In *The Culture of Disbelief,* the renowned constitutional lawyer Stephan Carter points out that American law and politics undercut religious devotion. He argues that it is the American habit to treat faith as a hobby: something to be done privately for a few hours a week, not something to live your life by. In a society that encourages consumption, achievement, and affluence, faith in things unseen is viewed as trivial or cause for suspicion.

Yet privately Americans believe. In 1990, the Gallup poll discovered that 78 percent of all Americans believed in Heaven, with four out of five believing they were destined to go there. Breaking out this number by income, age, education, or gender does not significantly change the percentage. One man in journalism—a profession known to attract skeptics—interrupted a conversation about something else entirely: "Jessye Norman will be singing Strauss," he mused, "but I don't know who will be playing sax." He was describing Heaven as he thought it would be. Without irony.

Freud believed that deep religiosity was neurotic, as do many psychiatrists today. Surely he is right that there are people who use religion and belief in Heaven to hide from or compensate for the pain dealt out by life. But as we've seen, knowledge of Heaven has the opposite effect on experiencers. Far from hiding from pain, they work with it. Besides, the yearning expressed in wish fulfillment does not mean that the thing wished for is not there.

In one of life's gentler jokes on Freud, C. G. Jung, Freud's leading disciple and then critic, had a near-death experience during a heart attack, which he later ranked as one of the most meaningful experiences of his life. As Jung reports it in his autobiography, *Memories, Dreams, and Reflections,* "It seemed to me I was high up in space. Far below I saw the globe of Earth bathed in a glorious blue light. Ahead of me I saw a shining temple and was drawn toward it. As I approached, a strange thing happened. I had the certainty I was about to enter an illuminated room and meet there all those people to whom I was beloved in reality. There I would understand at last the meaning of my life."[2] Jung then felt himself being pulled back into his body. His doctor had just injected him with a powerful heart stimulant.

In a BBC interview in the 1970s, Jung was asked if he believed in God. He answered just like the experiencer that he was: "I don't believe, I know." In that decade when behaviorist B. F. Skinner reigned, it was remarkable that anyone connected with psychology had the clarity to affirm spiritual truth.

Science has been at odds with faith in Heaven since Newton convinced most of the modern world that for something to be true, it had to be predictable, measurable, and/or repeatable. But a recent wave of books by reputable scientists has argued that astrophysics and quantum mechanics can be used to prove the existence of various aspects of metaphysics.[3] Once the existence of dimensions outside the ones we "know" can be established, there is all the room in the world for Heaven.

Medicine, that foot soldier of science, has also begun to acknowledge and even provide evidence of the spiritual truths that near-death experiences are pointing to. It was a skeptical resident who found the red shoe on the roof of Hartford Hospital because a patient on the ground floor claimed it was there after her near-death experience. A renowned cardiologist was the one who discovered that cardiac-arrest patients who had NDEs were the only ones who could describe the resuscitation effort without a single error. What does it mean when a soul can gather information separate from the limitations of body?

Twentieth-century thinking has brought us to the mistaken idea that people are like appliances. As long as we are plugged in, the television is active and filled with energy and action. Unplugged we are nothing. But the question essential to our humanity is: What is life energy and what is its source? The stories of near-death experiencers suggest that our life power, the energy of souls, has a consciousness and an identity that survives and thrives separately from the limitations of our bodies. If our souls can exist in another realm than the material, then souls can participate in life after physical death.

So what has fogged up faith in Heaven? We each bear the weight of individual doubt. Suppose, for example, that someone was brought up in a strict, judgmental church where the threat of hell meant living life with the constant anxiety of the punishment that might be coming. Such a person could well decide there is no afterlife rather than tolerate that anxiety. Many people look forward to seeing those they love in Heaven. But suppose one's deceased father was abusive, either sexually or violently. Someone with such a father might not yearn for a reunion with family members in Heaven. Or suppose someone has never experienced unconditional love; the notion of being in the presence of perfect happiness may seem impossible.

A minister tells the story of visiting a woman in her nineties who knew she was going to die soon. He said, "Isn't it comforting to know as a Christian that you'll be going to Heaven?"

The old woman told her pastor that she did not believe in Heaven anymore. It seemed that she had been married twice, both times happily. She would rather not go to Heaven than have to choose between the two men. Her minister reminded her of the parable of the woman who had been married seven times in which Jesus says that, in Heaven, we are not given or taken in marriage. The dying widow listened intently and then said, "Okay, I guess I'll go."[4]

Our doubts, while deeply felt, are often circumstantial. Each barrier is created by our individual realities and has little to do with Heaven's ultimate reality.

We all doubt our worthiness for Heaven. Each one of us knows in our innermost heart some deed or character flaw that could exclude us. But the life reviews of experiencers suggest that becoming aware and learning from our mistakes, not judgment, is our task. No more pure or holy than any one of us, experiencers bear witness to the fact that no matter what our guilty secrets, we will all be welcomed.

All over the world, in religions throughout time, people have believed in Heaven. We should take the wide range of human belief in Heaven seriously. There is something in us that gravitates toward the truth.

We have many ways of learning the truth. Logical or emotional truth, intuitive or demonstrated truth: they are all ways of knowing and believing. Human beings affirm Heaven not just because we want to escape the fact of death, but also because so many of us have experienced the reality of things unseen and confirmed in our own way the rumor of heaven. Think of Carolyn Wardner listening to the chimes of her clock ring a hundred times the minute her mother died across town. Think of George Jehn seeing his deceased best friend with a full head of hair and Lehman Woods describing accurately anesthesiologists he never saw. The religious beliefs and the broad heritage about Heaven are not some collection of theories invented by vastly imaginative priest figures. Beliefs about the afterlife are a complex alchemy of religious legacy, visions, dreams, intuitions, and experiences of reasonable people that have led to the widespread sense that Heaven is real.

A glimpse of Heaven's light creates significant changes in experiencers' lives. Mary Pollak gave up alcoholism. Diana Wood learned to deal with her difficult family. Steve Miner let go of his self-destructive impulses. They were all transformed by the experience of unconditional love. There's the self-absorbed newlywed who becomes a caregiver for the elderly. There's the ambitious athlete who now believes that only love, not winning, matters. And perhaps most significant of all, there's the absolute clarity and joy these experiencers and all experiencers have, that someday they will participate in a blissful afterlife. These aftereffects are the practical evidence in the case for Heaven.

We don't have to be an experiencer to learn the lessons of Heaven experiencers tell. Often when people first learn about near-death experiences they realize that important moments in their family's spiritual lives were nearing-death awareness or near-death experiences, but had not been seen as such. Phyllis Boucher is part of an extended family who were all touched by Heaven through the death of her three-year-old niece, Marjorie Mason. Midgie, as she was called, had a terrible, degenerative disease that caused her fingers and toes to wither and fall off. She was remarkably sweet natured about her disease. She used to say to her mother, "Aren't you glad I have my fumbs [sic]?"

The day before Midgie died, her mother came in to her after her nap and was taken with the joyful look on her little daughter's face: "Midgie, sweetheart, you look so happy."

The little girl looked up at her mother and said, "I've been to play in God's garden, Mummy. It was so, so beautiful there. He said I could come back to play tomorrow. You won't mind, will you, Mummy?"

She died the next day. Midgie's mother lost two more daughters, one to cancer and one to suicide. She told the story of Midgie's time in God's garden over and over throughout her life of terrible loss.

Midgie's near-death visit to God's garden was more than a great blessing. It also acted as a private source of revelation. To paraphrase H. Richard Niebuhr, one of the greatest Protestant theologians of the twentieth century, revelation is that moment in which we know ourselves to be known by God, and when God chooses to make Him or Herself known to us. Niebuhr goes on to say that revelation means "the moment in which we are surprised by the knowledge of someone there in the darkness and the void of human life; it means the self-disclosure of light in our darkness."[5]

Even the recent revision of the catechism of the Catholic Church, cited because it is a relatively conservative text, acknowledges that personal revelation is possible in the twentieth century. The relevant passage indicates that even though revelation through Christ is complete, "private revelation may help us live more fully by it in a certain period of history."[6]

Religious history goes in cycles of revelation and law. Moses received the revelation of the burning bush in which God described his relationship to Moses' people and laid out the laws by which he wanted them to live. It then became the task of the community to codify and abide by what Moses had learned. Revelation tends to appear when present religious law no longer resonates with Spirit. Jesus, for example, was a source of revelation in an era of zealous legalism among the Sadducees and Pharisees, the religious leaders of their time. Jesus and his revelations challenged the religious establishment and infused new Spirit into the religious code. In the Reformation, too, Luther's revelation challenged a church that was losing its connectedness to God.

A similar upheaval is at work today, but the nature of the messengers had to change. If an Ezekiel or a Muhammad were in the world now, he might make it to the newspaper tabloids. If he were media shrewd, one of the talk shows might let him share his convictions. But more likely he would end up in a psychiatric unit diagnosed as delusional. So the nature of revelation had to change. It had to be diffused. Instead of one person coming down from the mountain with two tablets, we have millions and millions of people catapulted to the edge of the ineffable and back again. Near-death experiencers are telling their family and friends what mystics through the millennia have always learned. This is not to imply that experiencers are mystics. The ability of modern medicine to bring people back from the brink of death means that literally millions of people who have not dedicated their lives to the spiritual path have been pushed into it. But experiencers do report what mystics have always reported: that God's Presence is awesome and beyond words, that we are supposed to love one another and ourselves, and that someday, when we die, we will go to be with God.[7] Near-death experiencers like Midgie function as a wellspring of collective religious revelation.

A wellspring. There is an ancient story, the origins of which are not known,[8] of a spring of water in the desert that had been there as long as Time. The spring was difficult for travelers to find, and someone finally thought to mark its presence with a stone. It became a tradition. Each traveler who came to the spring and marveled at its presence would place a stone there. After a while the stones covered the spring. Still travelers would stop, listen to the gurgling sound of water beneath the stones, and add one more stone to acknowledge the miracle of water in the desert. Soon there were so many stones, travelers could no longer hear the water. But still they added stones. It was a tradition.

Time went by. No one could remember why the heap of beautiful stones was in a pile in the desert.

Faith for many today is like those stones. Religious life seems parched, even dried up. Each near-death experience acts to lift a stone off the pile, bringing us one testimony closer to rediscovering the wellspring of all religions, all through time.

Heaven has been described as surrounded by the vineyards of religion, science, and near-death experiences. But there is a fourth vineyard on the edge of Heaven, which is faith. Faith in the original Greek has two aspects: *gnosis*, to know, and *pistus* to trust. Not all of us have been given the joyful certainty about the afterlife that experiencers have. But we can, in the light of their certainty, make a decision to trust.

It has been said that the central task of life is to accept a series of losses: the loss of our youth, and then of our children, the loss of our work, and then of life itself. This paradigm seems very brave. It describes the way things are, and therefore seems wise. But the testimony of experiencers contradicts this attitude. They affirm life as a precious gift. For every loss, there is a gain of such magnitude that it overshadows the loss. The loss of our youth brings a gain in maturity. In letting go our children we gain a measure of freedom and the chance to be an individual that we did not have during the child-raising years. When we no longer work, there is added time to savor the goodness of life and, one hopes, reap some of the rewards of our labor. The pros and cons of any of these stages should not be sugarcoated. Old age is not for sissies. But all of life does take on a different cast when we decide to trust that in shedding this world at death, we gain a life after life that is Heaven.

We all make decisions to trust all the time: when we marry, or send our children off to college, change jobs, or sell the house we have lived in all our lives to retire. We make those decisions with incomplete information. Believing in Heaven is no exception. Our future in God's dwelling place cannot be proven. But the evidence is persuasive. Science no longer contradicts faith, and so many rich religious traditions provide a road. Eight million people in America alone, each with stories as richly compelling as the ones described here, believe that each one of them has traveled to the edge of the afterlife. That is an abundance of evidence. This very abundance is an invitation to live the pain and the joy and the heroism that our lives bring us, knowing and trusting that someday our souls will travel where bodies cannot, to dwell in great beauty and love in reunion with those we love who have gone before. Nothing can separate us from God's love. We have the promise of Heaven.

NOTES

1. Jon 2:6
2. Aniela Jaffe, ed., *Memories, Dreams, Reflections* (New York: 1965).
3. In October 1994, the *Wall Street Journal* devoted its book review column to three books "At the Intersection of Science and Religion," as the headline proclaimed. I take this to be a strong indication that interest in the reconciliation of those two subjects has gone mainstream.
4. I heard this story from Rev. Jim Kidd.
5. H. Richard Niebuhr, *The Meaning of Revelation*, pp. 152–153. This is a difficult book worth the work. I recommend it highly for anyone who wishes to delve more deeply into the notion of revelation. Also read the "First Lecture" in Gershom Sholem's *Major Trends in Jewish Mysticism*.
6. *Catechism of the Catholic Church*, p. 23.
7. For an excellent discussion of the differences between mystics and near-death experiencers, read Judith Cressey's *The Near-Death Experience: Mysticism or Madness*.
8. I heard this story from Nancy Evans Bush.

Epilogue: A Candle

When I was nine years old, my parents took my sister and me into Chartres Cathedral in France. To the right of the altar stood row upon row of candles. They looked like a stacked bank of glowing flowers, shimmering in the cool dark of the enormous cathedral.

My mother explained that Catholics believe that lighting a candle and saying a prayer for people they love who have died would help the people they love get into Heaven.

I am not a Catholic, but I thought this idea was wonderful. I still do. It is a wise ritual for loss. It commemorates, and it eases pain with the hope of being helpful.

Writing this book was not always easy. Especially in the beginning, there were days when I thought I was foolish to think I could write a book on a subject nobody was expert on. One day, when I was swamped with doubt, I wrote down a list. I called it the Candle:

> Lisa Rimmer
> Ruth Grobe
> Tom Siebens
> Sara Hadden
> Rie Yarnall
> Isabel Baker
> Wick Sloane
> Jim and Joann Kidd
> Meg and John Harkins
> Brenda Townsend
> Lisa Getman
> Frank Chapman
> my father

Some are people who have died whom I love. Others are people I love who have suffered the death of someone who shouldn't have died. Some are children who lost their parents too young; others are parents who lost their children. Two are afraid of dying. Every day I have looked at this list. Days when I was frightened I had nothing to say, days when I wanted to be with my children instead, days when laziness or self-doubt made me want to get up and leave, the candle reminded me why I was writing. This book is dedicated to them.

Heaven: A Bibliography

ARMSTRONG, KAREN. *A History of God.* New York: Knopf, 1993.

ATWATER, P. M. H. *Coming Back to Life: The Aftereffects of the Near-Death Experience.* New York: Dodd, Mead Company, 1988.

BADHAM, PAUL AND LINDA, *Death and Immortality in Religions of the World.* New York: Paragon House, 1987.

BECKER, ERNEST. *The Denial of Death.* New York: The Free Press, 1973.

BELLAH, ROBERT N. ET AL. *Habits of the Heart.* Berkeley, Calif.: University of California Press, 1985.

Bible, New Revised Standard Edition.

BORG, MARCUS J. *Jesus: A New Vision.* New York: Harper & Row, 1987.

BRONOWSKI, J., AND BRUCE MAZLISH. *The Western Intellectual Tradition, from Leonardo to Hegel.* New York: 1960.

BUDGE, WALLIS E. H. *The Egyptian Book of the Dead.* LaSalle, Ill.: Open Court Paperbacks, 1974, reprint.

BURNHAM, SOPHY. *A Book of Angels.* New York: Ballantine, 1990.

CALLANAN, MAGGIE, AND PATRICIA KELLEY. *Final Gifts.* New York: Poseidon Press, 1992. Bantam reprint, 1993.

CAPRA, FRITJOF. *The Tao of Physics.* Boulder, Colo.: Shambala, 1975.

CARTER, STEPHAN L. *The Culture of Disbelief.* New York: Basic Books, 1993.

Catechism of the Catholic Church. Mahwah, N. J.: Paulist Press, 1994.

CHURCH, FORRESTER F. *Entertaining Angels.* San Francisco: Harper & Row, 1987.

CRESSY, JUDITH. *The Near-Death Experience: Mysticism or Madness.* Hanover, Mass.: Christopher Publishing, 1994.

CULLMANN, OSCAR. *Immortality and Resurrection.* New York: Macmillan ,1965.

DEANE, ANTHONY. *The World Christ Knew.* East Lansing, Mich.: Michigan State College Press, 1953.

DEWOLF, HAROLD L. *Eternal Life: Why We Believe.* Philadelphia: Westminster Press, 1980.

DOSSEY, LARRY. *Meaning and Medicine.* New York: Bantam, 1991.

ELIADE, MIRCEA, editor in chief. *Death, Afterlife, and the Soul.* New York: Macmillan, 1987.

————. *The Sacred and the Profane.* New York: Harvest Books, a division of Harcourt Brace & Company, 1987, reprint.

FERRIS, TIMOTHY. *Coming of Age in the Milky Way.* New York: William Morrow & Co., 1988.

FOWLER, JAMES W. *Stages of Faith.* San Francisco: Harper & Row, 1981.

FOX, MATTHEW. *Original Blessing.* Santa Fe, N. M.: Bear & Company, 1983.

FREMANTLE, FRANCESCA AND CHÖGYAM TRUNGPA. *Tibetan Book of the Dead.* Boston: Shambala, 1975.

FREUD, SIGMUND. *A General Introduction to Psychoanalysis.* New York: Washington Square Press, reprint, 1952.

GALLUP, GEORGE JR., WITH WILLIAM PROCTOR. *Adventures in Immortality.* New York: McGraw-Hill, 1982.

GLUBB, SIR JOHN. *The Life and Times of Muhammad.* New York: Stein and Day, 1970.

GOLDMAN, ARI L. *The Search for God at Harvard.* New York: Times Books, 1991.

GROF, STANISLAV, AND CHRISTINA GROF. *Beyond Death.* New York: Thames and Hudson, 1980.

HARPUR, TOM. *Life after Death.* Toronto: McClelland & Stewart, Inc., 1991.

HARRIS, BARBARA. *Full Circle.* New York: Pocket Books, 1990.

HARRISON, EDWARD. *Masks of the Universe.* New York: Macmillan, 1985.

HAWKING, STEPHEN W. *A Brief History of Time.* New York: Bantam, 1988.

HICK, JOHN H. *Death and Eternal Life.* New York: Harper & Row, 1976.

HOFFMAN, EDWARD. *The Way of Splendor.* New York: Random House, 1981, reprint.

HUXLEY, ALDOUS. *Heaven and Hell*. New York: Harper, 1955.

JACOBS, LOUIS, ed. *Jewish Mystics*. London: Kyle Cathie, 1990.

――――. *What Does Judaism Say About . . . ?* New York: Quadrangle, 1973.

JAMES, WILLIAM. *The Varieties of Religious Experience*. New York: Longmans, Green & Co., 1902.

JUNG, CARL. *Memories, Dreams, Reflections*. New York: Random House, 1961.

Kabbalah. Translated by Gershom Scholem. New York: New American Library, 1978.

KATZ, JAY. *The Silent World of Doctors and Patients*. New York: Free Press, 1984.

KELSEY, MORTON. *Afterlife*. New York: Paulist Press, 1979.

KÜBLER-ROSS, ELISABETH. *On Death and Dying*. New York: Macmillan, 1969.

KUNG, HANS. *Eternal Life*. Garden City, New York: Doubleday, 1984.

――――. *Freud and the Problem of God*. New York: Doubleday, 1979.

KUSHNER, LAWRENCE. *Honey from the Rock*. New York: Harper & Row, 1977.

LEWIS, C. S. *The Great Divorce*. New York: Macmillan, 1946.

――――. *A Grief Observed*. New York: Seabury Press, 1961.

LINGS, MARTIN. *Muhammad: His Life Based on the Earliest Sources*. New York: Inner Traditions International, 1983.

MACGREGOR, GEDDES. *Images of Afterlife*. New York: Paragon House, 1992.

MARSDEN, GEORGE, ed. *Evangelicalism and Modern America*. Grand Rapids, Mich.: Eerdman, 1984.

MASLOW, A. H. *Religions, Values and Peak-Experiences*. New York: Viking, 1970, reprint Arkana, 1994.

MCDANNELL, COLLEEN, AND BERNHARD LANG. *Heaven, A History*. New Haven: Yale University Press, 1988, reprint Vintage Books, 1990.

MCINERNY, RALPH. *St. Thomas Aquinas*. South Bend, Ind.: University of Notre Dame Press, 1977.

MCLOUGHLIN, WILLIAM G. *Revivals, Awakenings, and Reform*. Chicago: University of Chicago Press, 1978.

MOODY, RAYMOND A. *Life after Life*. Harrisburg, Pa.: Stackpole Books, 1976.

――――. *The Light Beyond*. New York: Bantam, 1988.

――――. *Reflections on Life after Life*. New York: Bantam, 1977.

MORSE, MELVIN. *Closer to the Light*. New York: Ivy Books, 1990.

――――. *Transformed by the Light*. New York: Villard Books, 1992.

NIEBUHR, H. RICHARD. *The Meaning of Revelation*. New York: Macmillan Company, 1941.

NIEBUHR, RICHARD R. *Resurrection and Historical Reason*. New York: Charles Scribner's Sons, 1957.

NULAND, SHERWIN B. *How We Die.* New York: Knopf, 1993.

OBAYASHI, HIROSHI. *Death and Afterlife: Perspectives of World Religions.* New York: Greenwood Press, 1992.

OSIS, KARLIS, AND ERLANDUR HARALDSSON. *At the Hour of Death.* New York: Avon, 1977.

PEGIS, ANTON C. *An Introduction to St. Thomas Aquinas.* New York: Modern Library Edition, 1965.

PHELPS, ELIZABETH STUART. *The Gates Ajar.* Boston: Fields, Osgood & Co., 1868. Reprint by Belknap Press of Harvard University Press, Boston, 1964.

PLATO. *Phaedo.* Translated by Harold North Fowler. Cambridge, Mass: Harvard University Press, 1938.

———. *The Republic.* Translated by Allan Bloom. New York: Basic Books, 1968.

RING, KENNETH. *Heading Toward Omega.* New York: William Morrow, 1984.

———. *Life at Death.* New York: Coward, McCann & Geoghegan, 1980.

RINPOCHE, SOGYAL. *The Tibetan Book of Living and Dying.* San Francisco: HarperCollins, 1992.

ROBINSON, J. A. T. *Honest to God.* Philadelphia: Westminster Press, 1963.

SABOM, MICHAEL B. *Recollections of Death.* New York: Harper & Row, 1982.

SCHOLEM, GERSHOM. *On the Kabbalah and Its Symbolism.* Translated by Ralph Manheim. New York: Schocken Books, 1964.

SCHUON, FRITJOF. *Dimensions of Islam.* London: George Allen & Unwin Ltd., 1970.

SMITH, HUSTON. *The Religions of Man.* New York: Harper & Row, 1986 copyright renewed.

SUTHERLAND, CHERIE. *Transformed by the Light.* Sydney, Australia: Bantam, 1992.

SWEDENBORG, EMANUEL. *Heaven and Hell.* New York: American-Swedenborg Printing & Publishing Society, 1883.

TILLICH, PAUL. *The Courage To Be.* New Haven: Yale University Press, 1952.

———. *Dynamics of Faith.* New York: Harper & Row, 1957.

TOON, PETER. *Longing for Heaven.* New York: Macmillan, 1986.

TURNER, ALICE K. *The History of Hell.* New York: Harcourt, Brace & Company, 1993.

VINCENT, KEN R. *Visions of God.* Burdett, New York: Larson Publications, 1994.

WEISS, BRIAN L. *Many Lives, Many Masters.* New York: Fireside Books, 1988.

WESTERMANN, CLAUS. *God's Angels Need No Wings.* Translated by David L. Scheidt. Philadelphia: Fortress Press, 1979.

WILDER, AMOS N. *Otherworldliness and theNew Testament.* New York: Harper & Row, 1954.

WILSON, PETER LAMBORN. *Angels.* London: Pantheon, 1980.

ZALESKI, CAROL. *Otherworld Journeys.* New York: Oxford University Press, 1987, reprint, 1988.

Zohar, volumes 1–5. Translated by Maurice Simon and Paul Leventoff. New York: Soncino Press, 1934.